After This

After This

10 Tips Moving Beyond Heartbreak

Melissa F Williams

Contents

Preface

SADLY, AND OFTEN, *in today's society, some have devalued the sacred reverence of marriage while minimizing the heartbreak, anguish, and grief of divorce. We, as a culture of people, gather to celebrate and salute a couple's formal lifetime presentation of commitment to enter into a covenant relationship with each other—what we call a wedding ceremony. Yet the very word divorce gathers no one to the arena or arms of the same individuals whose union was once celebrated. The simple aroma of the announcement of an engagement brings an enormous outpouring of support, love, excitement, and joy. Most often, people with diverse backgrounds and cultures come together simply to witness the blissful couple and their lavish sacrament, a marriage ceremony. However, the demeaning connotation of the word divorce pushes the same diverse people into separate corners, as if they are in a boxing ring. This shameful and, for many, humiliating word divorce sometimes divides friends and families as if they are supposed to take sides. The mere thought of "love versus hate" tends to be silent and unspoken but often loud, boisterous, and shattering in facing reality to the lives of the same "blissful couple," from people who formerly gave a standing ovation that signified their approval of an agreement with the union.*

Divorce merges loneliness, grief, and failure together like a tornado.

A tornado extends from a thunderstorm to the ground, creating damaging paths full of visual evidence of uprooted trees and shattered homes destroyed by winds up to three hundred miles per hour. Some tornadoes are clearly visible, but rain or nearby low-hanging clouds obscure others. Tornadoes develop so rapidly that little, if any, warning is possible. Before a tornado hits, the wind might be calm and the air very still. It's not uncommon to see clear, sunlit skies behind a tornado. *My goal is to open the eyes of the reader as to how devastating a divorce can be to so many lives, just like a tornado, metaphorically speaking. The individual's inner turmoil can produce rapid outbreaks of emotions without warnings, similar to the calm wind and still air before a tornado. However, the setting of an oncoming divorce can develop so rapidly that little to no warning is possible. Neither "meteorologist," the husband nor the wife, saw the marriage ending while standing at the wedding altar. Yet too many indifferent "climate changes" in the marriage—or unresponsive, overlooked needs or hurts—can produce a life-changing windstorm called divorce. As with any form of devastation, this unfolding propels some individuals into regret or depression and others into joy and peace, depending on the marital relationship. But just as a tornado causes reckless destruction and damage, there are a rainbow of colors and bright skies "after this."*

It is my heart's desire that the pages of substance I share will bring joy and strategies to move you forward in life. Proverbs 8:33 (NIV) says, "Listen to my instruction and be wise: do not disregard it."

After this *is a profound statement you can quote and believe in, and perhaps it will impel you to love again instead of remaining in silent regression while going to a therapist and living a life of regret. However, my recommendation is for you to allow the pages of this manuscript to inspire forgiveness and restoration as you walk through the rest of your life to fulfill God's great destiny for you.*

After this *encourages moving beyond the heartbreak.*

Introduction

PEOPLE WHO HAVE experienced or suffered any form of heartbreak, perhaps feeling love has let them down, will have "after this" moments—whether you loved and a partner in turn left you, or you're the individual who loved and chose to walk out of someone's life for whatever the reason. I want to introduce you to a word: process. Process can take us all by surprise, simply because we don't know when it's going to rear its head or what to expect from it. I always say that process introduces procedures, and procedures introduce you to patience. To develop all three—process, procedures, and patience—you sometimes start with a problem. The process will reveal to you two areas that prepare you for the journey: strength and weakness. These two characteristics will help you develop for the next phase of your life as a whole person.

Psalm 138:8 (KJV) says, "The Lord will perfect that which concerneth me." In this text God does not share with David the detailed plan or give him the agenda, nor does he give visible or clear examples as to how His plan for David's life is going to unveil, but He gives the life-changing end results—that He, the Lord, will perfect David's life, meaning He will not abandon the works of a person's hands nor ignore the longing to fulfill and discover His plan for the lives of believers. God will perfect all that concerns you, and any level of anxiety or unease to you, GOD is perfecting you in the process, making you perfect for your next assignment. My prayer is that, on this course, you identify and take mental notes of both your strengths and weaknesses. Familiarizing yourself with these opposites can be the driving force to your unknown potential or the gift for the call of God in your life. Identifying your strengths and weaknesses then allows you to release them. They also can work for you if you allow them *to develop you. Embracing your strengths and weakness can prepare you for life, business, relationships, and destiny, while introducing you to purpose.*

All of you be submissive to one another and be clothed with humility, for "God resists the proud, but gives grace to the humble. Identifying them then allows you to release them. Therefore humble yourselves under the mighty hand of God, that He may exalt you in due time, casting all your cares upon Him, for He cares" (1 Peter 5:5–7 NKJV).

Casting all your cares on God gives you the ability to remain persistent on your journey. To press forward, you cannot carry dead, burdensome weights. Hebrews 12:1 (NLT) instructs us, "Let us strip off every weight that slows us down…And let us run with endurance." While you are going through the process, weights such as regret and pain from a breakup can instantly slow you down and keep you from finishing strong. Can you imagine running a marathon with fifty-pound ankle weights? It would be extremely hard to produce speed or gain enough momentum to make mileage, let alone finish and win. It's amazing how many people in the tiresome race of life fail to see the two elements that are weighing them down: care and concern. Those very things weighed down the ten spies who didn't finish strong. Remember what happened when the Israelites reached the Promised Land? They had just been rescued out of four hundred years of slavery. They had walked through the Red Sea and had watched the Egyptian army drown. They had been miraculously guided through the wilderness and had been promised a land flowing with milk and honey. Miracle after miracle, blessing after blessing, all they had to do was trust and obey God.

Heavy concern regarding the possible danger to their wives and children kept them from moving forward in God's promise to do His will. It's vitally important that I clarify that our families, friends, and marriages are not the weight—it's the concern for them that becomes the weight. If we doubt or question God's desire and ability to heal, take care of us, or provide for us, we disregard His integrity and strength. It's interesting to recall that Caleb and Joshua eventually proved the error of their generation, forty years later, when they indeed went to battle with the same Canaanites and the Israelites were not harmed in any way. In fact, doing battle actually blessed their wives and children by giving them a fruitful land for their inheritance. The spies who fought to protect their families ended with nothing. But the two leaders, Caleb and Joshua, believed and trusted God, obeying Him at His word and inheriting the Promised Land filled with milk and honey. It was their destiny. By simply casting their cares on God and trusting Him, they could live in a new place of purpose and provision. The weighted cares and concern of the family were surrendered to God, and thus not only were their families blessed, but another generation also benefited.

So your marriage has ended in divorce, and your relationship with a significant other is over—now what? You must cast all of these weights on the Lord. The result will benefit not only you but also another generation that prayerfully will not have to experience divorce. They will be the leaders who stand and receive the power of God's purpose for their lives in loving marriages. This book is designed to empower and motivate you to move into the next season of your life. I want to remind you that with every relationship are a lesson—and with every hurt there is awakening. Don't turn a lesson learned into a soul mate.

Believe it or not, pain produces purpose. You might not see it or understand it, but a tutorial is in the making, one that will help you uncover the diamond in the ashes and will equip you, the new general, rising from the pain of war. Allow the pain of yesterday to reveal the greatest strength for the journeys of today and tomorrow.

Pain provokes purpose to stand—your destiny is waiting for you to take a stand.

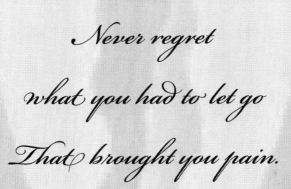

Never regret

what you had to let go

That brought you pain.

TIP 1

~~~

Face the Truth

AFTER JOB HAD prayed for his friends, *the Lord restored his fortunes and gave him twice as much as he had before. All his brothers and sisters and everyone who had known him before came and ate with him in his house. They comforted and consoled him over all the trouble the Lord had brought on him, and each one gave him a piece of silver and a gold ring.*

The Lord blessed the latter part of Job's life more than the former part. *He had fourteen thousand sheep, six thousand camels, a thousand yoke of oxen and a thousand donkeys. And he also had seven sons and three daughters. The first daughter he named Jemimah, the second Keziah and the third Keren-Happuch. Nowhere in all the land were there found women as beautiful as Job's daughters and their father granted them an inheritance along with their* brothers.

After this, **Job lived** *a hundred and forty years; he saw his children and their children to the fourth generation. And so Job died an old man and full of years.*

—Job 42:10–16 (NIV)

The book of Job contains the lengthy dialogue of several individuals on the nature and actions of God. What's compiled between the action of the first two chapters and final chapters is mind blowing. This book of conversations poses questions but reveals truth in action. Whether the book of Job gives satisfactory closure to all the pain, agony, and hurt Job had experienced, well, that depends on your perspective. However, the book of Job captures and presents the true power of loss and gain, death and life, and patience despite troubles, illustrating for us a story of encouragement to follow as an example in our lives. The

1

true heartfelt yet overwhelming story of Job adds an entirely new meaning to the phrase **the half hasn't been told.** It also marks an earned applause for the endurance of Job, while giving a glimpse of the restoration of Job's family and prosperity. The remarkable truth I want to covey to you is hope. Whether any event in your life was part of the plan of God or a result of your bad choices, there is hope **"after this"** for all. As many know the story, Job suffered for the glory of God, as do many of us. He holds fast to his patience and confidence in God, and then in his "after this" moment, God gives him double. In this momentous story of our brother Job, the text says, **"After this, Job lived..."** After all the unthinkable incidents, accidents, death, gut-wrenching heartache, enormous suffering, and tremendous loss that took place in his life, Job found a place of peace amid this turning point. If you can find a nugget of peace, a reason to still worship, or a glimpse of hope to continue this journey called life, you too will have an "after this" moment.

The saddest, most selfish moment in your life would be to simply survive or exist and never make some sort of mark on the earth, to never grasp self-worth or your life's purpose from within. Regardless of life's trials and disappointments, one thing is for sure: LIFE happens to us all, and for many it's called a divorce, a bad breakup, or a split. To you, this form of ache or pain poses questions about who you are as a person, wife, husband, lover, or friend, whether in covenant or simple platonic relations. The question you ask yourself really becomes, who am I as my identity pertains to relationships? You have to be true to you and understand that the only person who has to be free to live and not merely survive is the one person in this unresolved heartache or puzzle—you. When you permit yourself to be truthful with yourself, you then step into ownership, responsibility, and boundaries. This is a moment in time when you just tell yourself the brutal truth.

Ownership, Responsibility, and Boundaries

Ownership, according to Merrian-Webster's dictionary, is the state of owning something. It is owning, accepting, acknowledging, and admitting that this is and that was. I own my part in this situation. But now, I have to own my emotions, choices, desires, and those I allow in my circle.

Responsibility, according to Merrian-Webster's dictionary, is something you do that is morally right or legally correct. It's the required task or duty expected from you. It's your responsibility as to how you handle this divorce or breakup with that person.

Boundaries, as stated in Merrian- Webster's dictionary, are imaginary lines that show where an area ends and begins. Boundaries are unofficial rules about what should not be done and limits that define acceptable behavior. It's also a point or limit that indicates where two things become different.

When we hear or use these words—ownership, responsibility, and boundaries—in our everyday lives, these are profound, strategic words that ultimately project action and demand attention. These words of declaration bring us into a place of self-authority, self-control, and self-permission. As a person facing the truth, you must identify with the responsibility of your actions and choices. Taking responsibility legitimizes your effort to feel the pain or hurt with no need to hide your true emotions. When a person has experienced love and loss in a relationship, sometimes there is self-blame. Within the subconscious mind, one asks, him- or herself questions that aren't always easily answered.

A person going through the dissolution of a relationship might allow him- or herself to be captivated by the thought of being loved and not the reality that this person is not deserving of his or her love due to his or her actions. As an individual you must take responsibility for yourself and own your thoughts to stop with the fairy tale of accepting or permitting yourself to be in a relationship in which you are not appreciated or valued. A person is undeserving of your love when you have given your all and he or she is abusing you mentally or physically. This person does not deserve your love in either a marriage or any other type of relationship. Love this person enough to get him or her help if he or she will allow you to. But do not do it at the cost of your life, because any form of abuse is not love. When you set boundaries, you are making it very clear as to what you will permit in your life and what you will not, and being abused should be one of these boundaries. It's really about knowing what you deserve. Taking the responsibility to walk away from an abusive relationship doesn't make you weak; it actually proves how strong you are. Everyone is deserving of unconditional love, despite past actions. But knowing when to love or leave is the determining factor of any relationship.

An uncertain or traumatic relationship is when you must put your boundaries in proper place. Only you know the value of your time, your love, and your being as a person. Only you can set the bar as to what's permissible in your life. A person who does not know how to say no or how to walk away from what's hurting is a person in self-denial. Now, don't get me wrong. Some people have beautiful, happy relationships in which the spouse or partner stayed and things worked out. I'm not saying that everyone needs to walk away if he or she is unhappy. What I'm conveying is every relationship is unique and must be handled as such. People should not assess their relationships on someone else's relationship, be it marriage or any other form of friendship. It will be unfair to the individual and the partner. I've witnessed many marriages that have been saved because of someone staying, praying, walking in faith, and believing that God would turn things around and that God would restore and heal their relationship. But I will say it takes both parties to want it to work because God can do it.

However, you must trust yourself to set boundaries against the toxic behavior of people. You cannot expect the zebra to change its stripes and become solid. It's a zebra! Once a person has shown you his or her true colors, don't try to repaint him or her. It is a waste of time and energy. You can only change yourself and your reactions to this person. However, it is completely true that a person can change his or her own ways. People will surprise you when you change your expectations of them and release them to the Lord. Sometimes it takes you walking away from a person or a situation for him or her to really identify that he or she also needs to change. The Bible says in 2 Corinthians 5:17, "Therefore if any man be in Christ, he is a new creature: old things are passed away; behold, all things are become new" (KJV).

So I admonish you to stand firmly in hope and faith and to be mindful of your own reactions to them. Know your boundaries and your limits in love, in business, and in any relationship. Write your boundaries down to remind you of your worth, your power, and your vision. When you know what you deserve, you will not settle for

4

anything less. When you know that you are deserving of peace and joy, you will do what it takes to maintain your peace and joy. It is a rewarding feeling to live a life that develops you mentally and emotionally. When you can look back over your life and see from where you have come from, it is an empowering moment. Living through life's experiences develops you in so many ways. You will realize that you have strength in areas where you thought you were weak. If you had not gone through these trials, you would never know the power of prayer. You would never know what it feels like to hurt, but now you're able to share your story with someone, and that will encourage that person that he or she too can and will also survive. I want you to know that no one should receive the total blame in a breakup. There are two people in a relationship, and trust me, if you talk to one person, he or she will have something to say about the other person that the first feels is a result of the relationship ending. If you don't take responsibility for your own actions, the more you see them, the more they become an action plan and principles for you to live by. Even releasing a significant other now from your life—because you are just realizing how he or she handles you hurts you—can be draining and cause you to feel downtrodden. When the effort of trying to be with someone consumes and depletes you emotionally, it's time to show that person the door. Release him or her from your future expectation so that he or she will give you what you deserve.

If he has already ruined your mascara,
Don't let him ruin your life.

"Go ahead and be angry. You do well to be angry—but don't use your anger as fuel for revenge. And don't stay angry. Don't go to bed angry. Don't give the Devil that kind of foothold in your life" (Ephesians 4:26–27 MSG).

I suggest that you be the classy and beautiful woman you are. Be the strong, tailored, and breathtaking man you have always been. In private, scream, cry, yell, throw darts at his or her picture if you need to as an emotional release—just don't stay there in that position of despair and hurt. Don't reside for long in a place of regret or anger. But know that you will propel to excel. This is not your end!

Sometimes the truth Can hurt, but the truth can also set you free.

Finally, tell yourself the truth…

The truth sounds like this, like the distress of a person who loved"?

"I feel I'm falling apart." "This hurts like hell." "I can't do this!" "God, I wish they would die." "How can he leave me for her?" "I can't believe I gave her all of me, and she would just do me like this." "What am I going to do with my life now?" "I thought we would be together forever." "I knew better—something told me before I married him." "Why did I fall in love with her?" "What's wrong with me?"

The preceding statements sound heart wrenching, right? Nevertheless, they reveal pain, fear, sorrow, hurt, anger, and rejection—all human emotions. They say for you, out of you, and to you, "I loved." They play a song of regret. They are preludes to a violin playing, "I'm sorry for me." This is the moment of truth when you can face the giant "this is my now" and deal with it all.

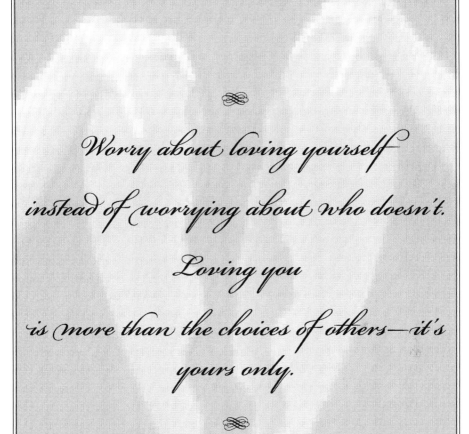

Worry about loving yourself
instead of worrying about who doesn't.
Loving you
is more than the choices of others—it's
yours only.

TIP 2

Be Transparent

Your transparency
is the window to your soul
and the breath of your existence.

TRANSPARENCY AS STATED *in Merriam-Webster's dictionary the ability to be seen through, honest and open—not secretive—and free from pretense or deceit.*

I will never forget the day my marriage ended. We were living in the same home, sleeping in the same bed, saying the same words to each other, but not "I love you" as often as needed. We had been inseparable (or so it seemed in the eyes of others). It appeared that he loved the very feet I walked on (in public). Besides, I was his wife, his "ride-or-die chick." When out with him, I often heard people who knew us, and even strangers, say to him, "You're a lucky man."

He always replied, "Yes, I am." These people spoke to him about my natural beauty, my heart, my outreach service in the community, my compassion for others, or my gift in ministering the Gospels or singing. Many times, when listening to or contemplating his reply to others, I felt baffled, like a deer in

9

headlights, just lost by his outward show of expression to another person regarding me.

Many times I found myself asking him, "Do you love me?" I often regretted having to ask for a show of affection from my then husband: "Can I have a hug or a kiss?" Sometimes I even asked, "Do I look nice?" or "Did you like what I had on today?" or "Did I do a good job ministering tonight?" At times, I questioned him: "Do you even like me?"

Please understand that you do not find for your self-worth in another person. That is a process of evaluating who you are and the things about you that you love and celebrate. Your self-worth is not measured by someone's accolades of you. That is just a generous bonus. Truly, your self-assurance and self-confidence lie within and exude outward. So as I share my personal experience, understand that I was not looking for him to build me. I was already a building standing tall and firm. I simply wanted him to show me that I was the apple of his eye. I sought to know he loved me, and as a spouse you desire your mate to love you without having to ask him or her. You long for your spouse to compliment you without your needing to ask. What the neglecting spouse fail to comprehend or haven't become conscious of is when they stop doing those things it makes the other person feel not loved, desired, or appealing to them. I want you to be assured of one thing: regardless of whether he or she "makes your head swell" with sweet, romantic words or complimenting expressions, know within yourself who you are, and you will eventually attract what your give and desire. Become your biggest cheerleader. Boost your own self-esteem by applauding your accomplishments and victories. Know that you are just as great, anointed, beautiful, smart, sharp, called and chosen, talented and confident even today as you where the day they stop recognizing it or fail to realize they had stopped. Remember what the Bible says in Psalm 139:14 (NIV): "I praise because I am fearfully and wonderfully made; your works are wonderful I know that full well." ***One thing we should do as believers is trust in the fact that God does not lie or makes mistakes. When He created you and me, He signed the approval and stamped it in His word to always remind us who we are to Him and in His eyes. With that truth you should have***

no doubt as to whom you are. Rest assured the Father loves you just the way you are.

It's sad to say or even admit, but the fun, outgoing person who loved outreach and ministry and who loved people is the person I was when he met me. He appeared to admire and love these qualities about me. But shortly after, it became apparent that those very same attributes were the things he had come to hate or not love and now wanted to change in relation to me once I said, "I do."

Nevertheless, when you realize your very significance, some people will say you shouldn't have to ask for compliments or affection from your spouse as long as you know who you are. I totally disagree with such a statement, as I explained previously. I feel that there should never be a moment when either spouse should beg or force the other to affirm or celebrate him or her. If he or she is not willing to spend quality time with you, give compliments freely, or even give of him- or herself freely, I strongly suggest the two have a heart to heart conversation. You would be surprised as to the love language they feel they are giving to you is enough. On the other hand, never make someone your priority when all you are to him or her is an option. Celebration and affirmation should be given freely when you are dating and should continue throughout your life together. However, please remember that you are the sum total of what you feel and think about you, from the inside to the outside. You're the best you, and when you know this others will freely celebrate and honor it.

One of the experiences I want to share with you opened my eyes in such a life-changing way. And I share this with you as maybe an eye-opening or a self-check moment. I loved my husband, yet in my heart, appearing in public, pretending to be a happy family, started to sadden me. From the outside, it appeared as if things were great on the home front. We were a beautiful black couple, both strong individuals with great goals and dreams we were pursing. Some would say that our marriage or blended family appeared successful in its own right, two successful people with the beautiful, well-mannered children and a nice home with a swimming pool. We attended church every Wednesday and Sunday. But little did outsiders know that my marriage was over. Honestly, and sadly, I don't think my husband even realized it. Some people, it seems, can just live in what others call dysfunction until it becomes the norm, and somewhere in their mind, it becomes right when it's been wrong since day one. Now I can't honestly say that I did not know his inner thoughts, but his actions spoke very loudly, so thunderous. I believed that such behavior is present in other people's lives, which is a form of dysfunction.

Yes, we lived in the same home but as parents, not as husband and wife. It felt like we were roommates. Now, the truly heartbreaking part about this is that we loved each other. We loved but not through wholeness. We loved but never really gave ourselves completely for many reasons. In retrospect, we believed we were. We were husband and wife, but we were like two strangers just being pleasingly polite to each other with "benefits." I mean no disrespect, but we couldn't love each other in fairness. At times I felt he loved me but didn't like me. What do I mean by that? Well, when you decide to enter into a covenant relationship with someone, you not only enter his or her present life but also his or her past and all its baggage, including joys, hurts, and happiness—the good, the bad, and the ugly. If a person has dealt with rejection, insecurities, and unstable family surroundings or comes from a dysfunctional" home with no visions or structured authority, it's very possible your marriage or relationship while traveling this journey called life will experience bumpy roads and turbulence while trying to take off.

Momma's Baby...Daddy's maybe

*It's easier to build strong children
than it is to repair broken men.
—Frederick Douglass*

12

For a man in the type of environment I mention earlier, he is ill prepared as a young boy to be a true man without struggling with his identity. This is just my opinion, because his being raised in a home with a single mother alone, and sometimes, she unknowingly tends to feel bad because Daddy isn't there. So she is more lenient in her discipline. He becomes used to getting all he wants from Mom and is never trained to be responsible or affectionate as a boy. In turn he grows up to become a mama's boy but a wife's responsibility and liability. Why? Because he was not raised by a father to be a son or a husband. Please understand that as a single mother myself, from my experience raising a son and a daughter I know that the needs, discipline, and guidance required for the two of them are different but are considered necessary.

To the many single mothers raising children, I salute you and honor you. It takes a very strong mother and woman to raise sons to be young responsible, hardworking, and respectful men in today's society. We see it not only being done successfully, but it is also a fact that mothers have to dig deeper to pour knowledge and discipline into our sons because we will never be a man, but we can prayerfully get wisdom from the Man of God. I know that too well. I pray that He gives us continuous wisdom so our sons will not be lacking in the area as mama's boys.

Sadly, in years past and even today, for some, there was no impartation of sonship, no impregnating conversations about real covenant versus convenience. Sadly, the truth about being a husband versus a lover for a night and not a lifetime was never discussed in the family home. This absence of training teaches and introduces to our sons that it's OK to desire having a woman but not a wife. The only image of a male role model was represented by the different uncles who came in and out of the home. The only thing that was instilled was teaching a son how to move from woman to woman, to run from responsibility, authentic love, and true compassion—a desire for sex and not love.

This type of representation introduces a false display about real-life relationships. It breathes the illusion to a male person that "love and sex are not commitments with just one woman" but that it's OK to be a nighttime lover and cheater and still be taken care of by his wife. If the mother was in church, the young boy saw the good reverend on Sundays. But that wasn't enough if the good reverend did not invest quality time beyond the pulpit.

For me as a wife, it was challenging to submit to a man who didn't have a clear understanding of the sanctity of marriage, and I found myself carrying the silent weight of the family. I carried the delegated but neglected position of a husband but in convenience the title and position of a wife. What I'm saying is I was put in a elected position that I did not run for to carry the family but maintain the requirements and expectations as a wife. Because of the lack of headship, my true position turned to ashes where there once stood a beautiful, charming, soft but strong woman who embraced with honor the role of being a wife. Now I sat, a woman burdened and broken in spirit, a wife waiting with poise in a room with beautiful flowers that were never touched by my hands because I was too busy trying to hold the family together until I missed the smell and gentle touch of a rose. But I carried in my hands the responsibility and vision of a family because somewhere in my heart I was destined to survive.

*Some women are
lost in the pain.
Some women are built from it.*

The four corners of those mortal bricks built to be a home then turned into a mere residence of heaviness and not happiness, peace, or togetherness. As the wife I carried the pressure of my husband, but I was created to bring him favor and to help him as a wife. I was birthed from the womb to be a giver and a seer, to speak prophetically regarding my home, to dream for him, to pray the assignment in heaven to manifest into the earth what was in his heart and spirit. I was never designed or created to have the vision for the family, but I was to pray, push, and support the visionary. I was anointed to listen and

intercede while watching to cover the vision. Women weren't given the gift in a marriage to be the visionary and of dreaming, plus building and making it a reality, in addition to bringing home the bacon and then having sex —out of order. Unless she is single – minus the sex part. Again, this is my opinion.

Sadly, this happens in many homes, yet we ask the question why there are so many single women today. However, being mindful of some women, their choice is to be single, and it's not a curse. And there is nothing wrong with that. Granted, today, and even in the church sector, in some marriages this type of man connects with women. He wants to walk in the order by the Word by being the head of the home but has no dominion in the earth. He demands dominion to rule and subdue in the home but not in the world. Again this is not speaking on marriage as if some fathers are not wonderful fathers and stay-at-home dads. This is not in reflection on those men. Many men/fathers—even stepdads—are doing an amazing job while the mother goes out to provide in another form for her family. Truthfully, we must salute them as well. Prior to marriage we must learn to discuss our expectations and our views as they relate to matrimony. Therefore, you will know before you say, "I do," what you are coming into agreement with. Sadly, and most often, we fail to ask the serious questions and fail to be truthful with ourselves as to what we want and don't desire. And in the end, it's not the spouse's fault as to why you are disappoint- ed. You never knew the truth because you didn't ask the right questions, share your true heart, or tell them your truth. A word of advice—even for me and for those who are willing to walk down this aisle again, first be truthful to yourself and secondly them. It will save a lot of hurt feelings and time wasted.

*Most of life's most impressionable mo-
ments happen when you are faced with*

challenges and pain that hurt but teaches you valuable lessons.

God blessed them; and God said to them, 'Be fruitful and multiply, and fill the earth, and subdue it; and rule over the fish of the sea and over the birds of the sky and over every living thing that moves on the earth'" (Genesis 1:28 NASB).

Now, please understand that I'm not saying a wife should not hold her husband down. That's exactly what I am not saying. Wives are helpers to their husbands, but please give us something to help with. I believe marriage is twofold. Give and take—I have your back and you have mine. All of God's people, male or female, deserve to be appreciated and cherished. I don't believe that if either spouse falls on hard times the other should just walk away. I believe both should stay to put the pieces back together. However, according to the text, a man should be fruitful and multiply, but if he has not been taught the knowledge of this principle, he will wander through life thinking this principle is just for him to keep having babies and more baby mamas. This is a prime example as to why it is vitally important to introduce manhood to a son via a distinguished gentleman of God, with authority, structure, balance, and vision. If not, it leaves him to teach himself or watch those who have no real values or work ethic and structure. If he were raised to let his mom take care of him and cater to his needs, then guidance and structure is needed. Many mothers make this mistake unconsciously. The son could go outside to play with his friends and, if he was athletic, that was his life. Yet his sister was inside being trained to be a wife and mother, educated to be responsible and to work hard. She was learning to keep a house, and studying to be smart and productive. She was being nurtured to be caring and forgiving, independent and strong. Nevertheless, for my brothers, the lack of imparting has revealed the nearly suicidal mission of the family structure in our culture and in our black communities.

The fact remains that our sons or men either were not taught or had no leader to embrace the moments in their lives in which they became change agents for the next generation. *Being transparent to oneself is telling the truth. A woman cannot teach a male how to be a man or husband. If the first woman in his life instilled selfishness and the misconception of love versus smothering, the wife will become just the other woman because this man will not know how to leave the breast of his mother to cleave to the heart and soul of his wife. Simply because his dependency was wrapped up in his mother's paying the car note, washing the car, rotating the wheels, getting the oil changed, never permitting him to drive, or not forcing him to stand on his own two feet because of a lack of a father at home. She was just being a mother. Now, the sad and transparent truth is the aftermath. We now have fully grown African American black men and women who do not know or think it is a problem to have only their moms and women in their lives to take care of them. (But, my sistas, permitting that is foolishness, but that is a whole other story for another chapter and another book.)*

A person that knows their Value will wait for what they deserve instead of wasting time on what is in their reach.

From Boys to Men

Sometimes a man enters a woman's life thinking he is ready for a commitment, simply because no one was in his life to enlighten or advise him of the concrete truth that he is wrong in many areas but so are women. The wrong man will pat a son on his back when a man with a father's heart will sit his son down and tells the raw truth. The wrong man condones cheating and relays this to a boy at an early age. A father teaches and lives as the primary example of loyalty and of respecting the value of young ladies. The wrong man teaches sons how to be controlling and that the man is the only one with an opinion and voice.

But the father's heart pours into the son the ability to submit under a lesser authority, to listen to a mom or woman when times are tough, especially when God has sent him a wife. He sent her with a prayer and word for the man. But no one gave him, when he was younger, the opportunity to fail or shed light on teaching him it's OK to fall and get back up. So now he's that same boy but an oversize version who does not have an ear to hear the truth. If Momma didn't see a problem, then why should his spouse, girlfriend, or significant other deem anything needs to change? This stems from being raised in a home without a father, structure, or examples of leadership in their daily lives. Subsequently, he does not know how to give love, compassion, or even simple compliments to a significant other. Because of what he was not taught, you have now married into a suitcase of issues.

Truth—being transparent, I knew we both deserved more from life and love. One night I could not sleep because I knew after endless conversations and countless more unspoken moments of restlessness that one of us had to make a decision. The transparency is that my husband was a great individual; an awesome, hardworking man with many talents and gifts; and an outstanding father and dedicated husband, and it might not make sense, but he wasn't for me. Someone can love you and never have the capacity to carry you. You can love someone, and it is unlikely to work if things are pushed under the rug. Does he ever really know you? Not your title in the church or the your being the CEO in the boardroom but the person who says, "Hey, I'm human, too," the person who says, "I just want you to love me and not what I do." It doesn't take anything from either of the two. All the things I saw in him then, I see today but as my friend. You have to be able to judge the relationships in your life and place them in their right category.

Some people who enter your life are just ushers escorting you from one place to another and then return to their posts. However, we in turn allow them to take the empty chair next to us, to sit in the row with us, to eat popcorn, to drink out of the same straw, and then tell them to hold our seat until we return from the ladies room. Most of us, if we tell the truth, have made bad choices because of emotional neglect or circumstances. Or we moved too quickly in relationships because we didn't take the proper time to know who we are, what we really desire, what our call to this world is, or we chose in our "now moment," which is a temporary state, what I call the wilderness. You're between there and here. (That's another chapter.)

Both men and women sometimes make decisions from where we are now and not for where we are destined to go. We've forgotten the need for patience. Patience will allow you to heal, to enter into a new level of understanding as to whom you are as a person. Many times we lose sight of who we are in relationships because the relationship becomes our primary focus. Be patient. Wait for a moment. Take advantage of this time in your life. You now have the freedom to learn new things about you, visit places you've only dreamed about. Allow patients to have its perfect work in you. This is quality time that you and God should fall so much in love until literally your date night should be with Him. Your preparing for the next chapter of your life is sitting on pause waiting on you to slow down and breath. Don't be in a hurry to meet the next guy. Introduce yourself to the new you, the patient one who's resting in the fact that this is a new season of your life. And when it's time, you should select for where you see yourself beyond your present and walk into your promise, which is the purpose-driven life. We make choices while we are in the wilderness (our low places) when it would be better to slow down and enjoy the journey to get to there. This includes encountering new people along the way. We do not make wise choices as to where we are going, so we try to see or create in people qualities they haven't developed. And we become frustrated with them when we made the choice. "After this" you should take this time to better yourself and not look for someone to make you feel better. This way you will be able to accept people the way they are, and if they are not for you, you have learned through patience and time how to walk away and still value them as a person.

The question is, why do you stay connected? Why stay connected to someone who's not assisting you in fulfilling your greatest potential in life? Why remain with someone who only sees you from your past and not where you're striving to go? Why be in a relationship with a person who is only tolerating you instead of celebrating you? Why love someone who does not return love because he or she has never received authentic love? He or she also deserves love but not at your expense.

The Price of Love should not cost you to file emotional bankruptcy.

Speaking of the expense of love, His love cup is full to the max, but He is drinking a different liquid. That is why it doesn't work for the two of you. He is giving you His best and is happy. What He has to give is a language that appears empty to you when really it is His best wine. You're just drinking out of two different glasses. And the truth is that He is not wrong—you just chose the wrong glass to sip out of. You desired a champagne glass from Bloomingdale's but settled for the plastic cup that looks real from Dollar Tree. Now, just because he wasn't your fine wine or cup of tea doesn't means he's not the Lipton for someone's else's taste buds. On the other hand why linger in a relationship with a person who does not see your worth or treasure your greatest? Why even choose someone who just doesn't desire to drink out of the same glass as you? Or smile from a pure, authentic place when he or she sees you just because he or she is in your presence and simply because you are you? The question is what do you want to sip while on your journey, peace, joy, and love or frustration and heartache? Since you have made the choice to move on, be confident in this decision and move forward. Never regret a decision you had to make for the betterment of you. I knew that if he and I were to be our best as parents and people of God, I had to make a decision: it was to divorce. It did not matter to me what people thought, said, or assumed. I was determined to live and not survive. You know you really love someone when you can let him or her go and allow him or her to soar. Selfless acts are what most of us are fearful of. We make life decisions based on other people's opinions.

The truth of the matter is that it's your life. The day you realize that there is more to life than titles or labels, you will move forward whether your title is single, married, or divorced. However, it takes you to be transparent with you.

*Never downgrade yourself to match the capacity of someone else. You'll be too low to soar.

Transparency is when you can see through the visible object clearly and it's still lovable—when you see all flaws, hang-ups, mistakes, and hurts. When you make a choice to be perfectly honest and transparent with yourself, you might realize this breakup was best for you. Now you can focus and pursue, and if relationships are in the future, you can be wise in your decision making. To thine own self be true. Before you choose or are chosen, decide to love yourself first. Wait for what you deserve; don't settle. Just be patient. .

The masterpiece may not be appearing
on the canvas

the way you saw it in the vision,

but keep using your God-given tools

to stroke, design, and create.

Keep the vision before you.

I promise that in the end,

the master's work of art will be
beautiful.

TIP 3

❧

Forgive

"For when you forgive other people when they sin against you, your heavenly Father will also forgive you."

—Matthew 6:14 (NIV)

FORGIVENESS IS THE *key to freedom. When you allow yourself to forgive, you are able to release people, situations, and pain from your heart. Nearly everyone has been hurt by the actions of someone, whether a spouse, a friend, a family member, or maybe a business partner. These wounds can leave mental and emotional scars and can sow seeds of bitterness and hate. The actions of someone might offend you, but you oppress yourself by not releasing the offense. Forgiveness doesn't mean you deny the pain or condone the other person's act toward you. It just means that you make a permanent pronouncement to let it go. If you need to decide every day, come to a decision daily, second by second, to just let it go. People can hold themselves in so much bondage simply because they think it actually matters to others if they don't forgive them. And it does not. Yes, it hurts. Yes, it might be wrong how they treated you or even ended the relationship. But forgiveness gives you permission to love again and move forward with your life. Forgiveness releases you from the trap of silent control. That liberation starts with you. You must not give away your power to be free. Novelist Miguel de Cervantes said, "Never stand begging for that which you have the power to earn." Why wait for something you already have the power to activate? All that you are, the greatness you possess, will be wasted on a failed* relationship. Your life is worth more than a hurt or disappointment. Don't confuse hurt for eternal damnation. Hurt is temporary. You can live past this and the incident! If you're in the worst season of your life, get ready—the best season is just around the corner; you just took a detour.

I'm reminded of a story in Luke, chapters 22–23. This was the time of the festival of unleavened bread, Passover. The story gives a very profound narrative regarding relationships and God's will for one's life. This is an astonishing and surprising chronicle in that the priest and teachers were trying to find a way to get rid of Jesus. But the text says in Luke 22:3 (NIV), "Then Satan entered Judas, called Iscariot, one of twelve." In an unbelievable twist to this commentary, the same person who had walked with Him, who had eaten with Him, was considered to be a son, was the very one who approached the elders to set up the actual stage and use a tool of intimate affection by a kiss to betray Jesus. There are so many revelations in this theme that I want you to pay close attention to. The actual timing and plot of this alleged attack was in the will of God for the fulfillment and purpose of Christ. It appears as though Judas was a scandalous friend by his actions. But the irony in the text is that, yes, Satan entered him, but I believe Judas gave him access. This is just my opinion.

The Bible says in 1 Peter 5:8 (KJV), "Your adversary the devil, as a roaring lion, walketh about, seeking whom he may devour." My belief is there are people walking with you that you have given illegal access to your life and Satan has entered. You have given him, the devil, and an open door to your life, not because of who those people are but because of who you are. Judas was just like some of the people who have betrayed you with a kiss. Yes, they've walked with you, eaten with you, and were intimate with you. However, they were used to execute the greatness in you. They are jealous of you because they saw you fall and get back up. They hate you because regardless of what they have heard or even have witnessed from your past. It has not stopped you from pursing your destiny. Many who are bystanders in your life are witnessing you go through this time of divorce or heartbreak and yet can't understand how you keep showing back up day after day still *looking good and holding your head up. Some are only with you for the fishes and the loaves, and as soon as an opportunity presents itself, they will kiss you.*

What I want you to gain from this outstanding story is that sometimes your so-called enemies have been positioned in your life to not kill you but push you to a place of praise, power, and purpose. Judas was positioned in the right time in Jesus's life, to help fulfill destiny. If Judas had not been a prisoner under arrest by Satan with permission from God, he could not be a vessel of betrayal and the crime scene could not have been reported. If whoever had not been in your life to betray you, hurt you, abandon you, you wouldn't know how anointed you are to walk away. You would not know how strong you are to move beyond grief to greatness.

If they had not kissed you, you wouldn't know how to discern lust from love. If you had not witnessed or been so closely involved with the assailant, you wouldn't know how to properly guard your heart and your circle. So instead of you being angry with the person or people you feel betrayed you, just know that that was their purpose in your life. You're so anointed—there is a superior and larger assignment in your life than where you are now. You are not some mediocre, common, average, ordinary, regular, typical individual. You are anointed by God to do great exploits. His hand is on your life, and that's how you know. Your "after this" is enormous! That's why you should now understand Job 13:15: "Though he slay me, yet will I trust in him."

> *It's easy to trust when you know who has your back! I can now say, according to Psalms 119:71 (NIV), that "it was good for me to be afflicted so that I might learn your decrees." God is always on my side! Trust and believe that it's easier to forgive when you recognize and know it's working for your good. Betrayal is a tool to teach you the power of forgiveness.*

Melissa F Williams

Forgiveness
is the chain breaker,
not
hate or resentment—
that's self-sabotage.

Jesus displays and lives his immaculate life for us to learn and live by this principle: "Forgive them, for they know not what they do." Judas was a witness and victim, not a convict. The enemy stole his identity, and Jesus gained access to a greater reward. You now have access to the promotion of your life, simply by forgiving. The more you hold on to resentment, you hold yourself in solitary confinement. You become a prisoner in your mind, which in turn controls your actions and your heart, the next step into slavery. Every slave has a master. Who would be yours? When someone you care about hurts you, you can hold on to anger, resentment, and thoughts of revenge or embrace forgiveness and move forward.

The truth is
that forgiveness
gives you permission to
love again.

28

Forgiveness is a commitment to a process of change.

The Reimbursement of Forgiveness

Healthier relationships

Greater spiritual and psychological well-being

Less anxiety, stress, and hostility

Lower blood pressure

Fewer symptoms of depression

Stronger immune system

Improved heart health

Higher self-esteem and self-worth

Ability to see clearly

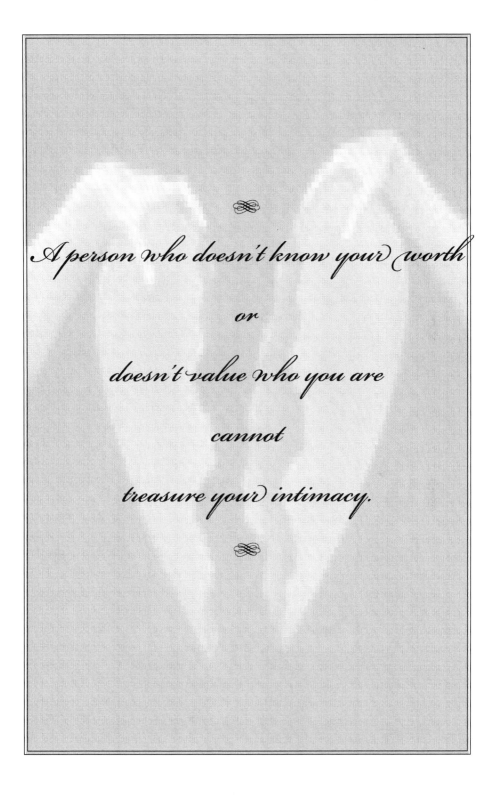

A person who doesn't know your worth

or

doesn't value who you are

cannot

treasure your intimacy.

TIP 4

❧

Loneliness

LONELINESS—THE RESIDUE OF *your past will lead you to...*

Often in life we make choices based on our perceived internal lack of wholeness, healing, and guidance. Many times, we internalize previous experiences and summarize them all to be the general rule. Life becomes a canvas of unfinished sketches or pictures, left undone. Our journeys become clay in our hands, waiting to be molded into a beautiful sculpture. We gather the pieces of life's puzzle and try to magnetically put them on a sliding board, never realizing that a puzzle has to be placed on a flat, solid surface to stay connected. Yet we continue trying to force the detached pieces together on a surface going downward. This is how we sometimes handle relationships—always trying to reattach what has detached from our lives and has us going in a downward direction. However, realize that every moment in life is an additional piece to the puzzle. We view life as a quiet yet stormy day, awaiting the appearance of the rainbow, only to be relieved to witness different color shades in comparison to our self-journey. Deep within, if we could relinquish hurts from the past, we could soar into places of positive expectation. We could witness the warmth and embrace the beauty in the colors and, at the same time, smile while living beyond where we started. The rainbow represents hope at the end of the storm—many colors, all representing a collection of diverse uniqueness. But what happens when all you can perceive is one color in the rainbow? What happens when all your feelings or emotions are bland? What if you were to wake up to life and realize you missed a world of liberation, joy, happiness, grace, and love? Some would say, "How could that be humanly possible, to just let life pass you by?" It is a fact that millions of people suffer from loneliness and the fear of being alone. It is called monophobia.

Monophobia is the extreme or abnormal fear of being alone. Many people, as well as animals, are known to suffer from monophobia, and it is not an easy fear to overcome. Monophobia is also known by other names, such as isolophobia or autophobia. It is characterized by extreme insecurity, anxiety, and depression when the person has to be alone, even for short duration. As a result, she or he refuses to sleep, eat, or even go to the bathroom alone. People suffering from monophobia are unable to do many simple tasks that most can do easily. The fear of being alone can also lead to bad relationships, as the individual prefers abuse to being left alone (to read this full article go to www.fearof.net)

Loneliness, as stated in Wikipedia, is a complex and unpleasant emotional response to isolation or lack of companionship. Loneliness is often accompanied by anxious feelings about lack of connectedness or togetherness with someone. Some might be surprised to learn that loneliness can happen even while you are connected to someone or surrounded by millions of people. This is how life can pass by swiftly, when you elude or avoid life and all its elements. You then enter a calm, serene, and yet disorderly world identified as loneliness.

When experiencing divorce or any form of disconnection, loneliness can live and be felt in the corridors of a person's mind and introduce questions about his or her self-worth or existence.

Loneliness

can be a secret escape from true emotions,

but never the pathway to true wholeness or

healing.

The causes of loneliness include social, emotional, and mental states. Research has shown that loneliness is present throughout marriages, divorce, or any form of relationships, as well as successful careers. Feeling lonely, being socially isolated, or being in solitude are clearly not the same. In particular, one way of thinking about loneliness is a discrepancy between one's desired and achieved levels of social interaction, whereas solitude is simply the lack of contact with people.

When your desire is solely centered on wanting to be with a particular person, whether right or wrong, your desire for companionship has taken the role of leader in your heart and emotions. And as it has been proved, your emotions can be a dangerous guide if not channeled and judged wisely. If they are sometimes based on your internal desires, your actions and intentions may not always match or agree. You then must become the moderator for your emotional significance. When an individual desires to be loved, held, or simply be in the presence of an individual, he or she sometimes overlooks, fails to notice, or neglects the process of gauging his or her emotional state and awareness, which is the most meaningful reward to being alone versus being lonely. Until loneliness is dealt with, the person will not fully know who he or she is, what he or she truly needs from a person, or the worth of loving him- or herself before giving love to another.

The best way to channel your desire is cited in Matthew 6:33 (KJV): **"Seek ye first the kingdom of God…and all these things shall be added unto you."** Your relationship with Christ has to be the ultimate love aspiration, target, and goal you desire before anything or anyone else. Then the desires of your heart will be equivalent to the desire God has for you. Your desire obviously can overshadow the separation between what you need and what you want. If loneliness is only being alone, it's then a matter of personal choice for some and an unexpected result for others. People can be lonely while in solitude or in the middle of a crowd. The number of people in someone's life does not indicate whether a person is lonely. That's why it is so difficult to see with the naked eye if someone you are close to is suffering. We judge or gauge a person's life based on his or her outward success or superficial lifestyle. Many people experience loneliness because of the absence of a particular person or the lifestyle the individual *presently lives. A person's lifestyle cannot fill the void or vacancy, permit true identity transparency, or fill the desire of the individual's depth of soul. There's a missing link to the puzzle. There's an unspoken lack of gratification, completeness, indulgence, or pleasure being met between the parties in the relationship. Whether it's in your career, an intimate bond, or a covenant relationship, a whisper of loneliness might be present. Conversely, one can be alone and never feel alone simply because there is no desire for social interaction.*

I remember a point when I was loving life. Wanting to be involved with someone was the furthest thought from my mind. My children were excellent and healthy, my ministry was growing, my business was excelling, my opportunities to venture into other business venues were on the rise, and many other areas of my life were expanding. I had even lost weight! I was a new person. Mind you, all these wonderful things were happening after my divorce. I wasn't where I wanted to be, but it sure felt good to be climbing the mountain.

When "Mr. Right" Shows Up

One day I suddenly was in the company of a brilliant black man who was very influential, and I didn't know it. One of my girlfriends had mentioned him to me, only suggesting that I listen to one of his sermons. So that was as much as I knew about him—his message. I had heard of this man maybe two months prior to actually meeting him, and, to my surprise, I was now at dinner with him and enjoying his company. (This was a total shock—being out to dinner, period.) Let me say that as a woman who hadn't been out on a date in a long, long, long time (plus infinity), I found it very nice, delightful, cozy, and fun. He was the perfect gentleman. As I sat next to him at the dinner table, I just looked at him, listened to his laugh, and thought to myself, "He's a cool guy and—oh, Jesus!—he smells sooo good!" (This woman was in a state of emergency.)

But within myself I was thinking, "Oh, Lord, why am I here?" My heart had been broken so badly that I had built an invisible wall. I was hesitant to let someone in, even just a male friend. Besides, I wasn't even considering dating again at this time—not that I didn't want someone, the right person, to eventually come behind the wall or into my private oasis and care enough to assist me with taking the wall down. I needed confirmation—it was time to permit and release, to permit myself to trust and feel safe again, to allow the protective walls to come down. And very soon after, this man of God said all the right things to assist me in that area. The walls that had secretly been built began to fall without making a sound or putting up a fight. He just wasn't aware of it.

However, I realized I had been brought back to life. I actually enjoyed his company. Never had I realized I was internally and emotionally in a coma, even though I believed I was just waiting for "Mr. Right." But I was so clueless, still unaware of the influence this man had on the earth until I sat and listened to his conversation. After a period of being in contact with him, I observed his life, which revealed his existence and assignment from God. It revealed to me his love for God and for God's people.

Observing him flow in his purpose allowed me to witness the heart of the person as an individual. Listening to others allowed me to witness his influence on the earth. But praying for him gave me access to a level of discernment and understanding as to who he was to God and the sensitivity in the realm of the spirit, allowing me to properly gauge between the man and the vessel. Last but not least, praying for him gave me permission and freedom to be me when dealing with him, because I now saw the heart of the person. So the people's preacher didn't impress or matter to me. I didn't want the people's preacher. I wanted to know him, the man eating the pizza and laughing, because he was just as human as I was. I preferred to know the person outside of the spotlight. I was out on a date with him, not with his position or title.

> *I wanted to know more about him as a person—what he liked, what made him cry, how to make him smile, and what he liked to do for fun so I could accompany him. I wanted to experience the rhythm of his heart and listen to his conversation so I could wisely weigh how to skillfully pray for him. And—oh my God!—I definitely needed to know what cologne he wore so I*

could stock up! Some time had passed, and I was still in communication with this outstanding guy. He was charming, handsome, cutting edge, revolutionary, and a priest of God, and he knew how to serve you a prophetic warrant. Whew! He came into my life and swept me off my feet.

Always be true to God and yourself about what your heart desires, and your sprit will discern if he or she is deserving of you.

However, this story isn't about him; it's about me. After time had passed and our communication continued, I realized I felt alone. It's funny how what to others is an obvious void in your life is something you don't miss, see, or feel until the right someone occupies that space even for a short time. Before I met him, I thought my life was finally coming together—as a single woman, that is. Then he showed up in my life. Boy, I wasn't expecting this.

The tough, solid, genuine truth is that I didn't realize I wanted someone or, in actuality, didn't care for being alone anymore—until him. Honestly, I enjoyed the thought of being with someone again because of him. If you're a woman like me, sometimes you don't want a titled relationship, the elementary labels of boyfriend and girlfriend. It's just nice to have someone there to share time and conversation with, "to kick it with," as they say—without all the stress of commitment and clingy neediness.

I wanted to have time to just enjoy the ride of a friendship that would build upon a foundational relationship. It was the essential opportunity to become friends before lovers. We as people sometimes miss out on this critical process all because we have a fear of being alone. And if he or she really is a keeper, we don't want that person to move on to another. So I totally understand the emotional drama of desire.

But what I want to suggest is a very simple rule or proposition: I propose that obtaining and keeping love is not about how sexy you are, how well you can dress, or how you become Ms. Nice who laughs at all his jokes. There are a million of these ladies out there. The number one rule is to be you—the secure, honest, walking-in-purpose, whole you. And number two, be his friend first. From experience, if a person is a catch or keeper, chasing him or her and being too forward or needy is a quick way to get him or her to exit.

You must allow the person to know and see you are a gift to his or her life, and that doesn't come through sex. How you present yourself and how a person perceive you and your actions is a guaranteed presentation to how they will treat you. When a person treats you in a way that you do not like If your silent about it is co-signing the approval document to them that this action towards me is permissible. Some women might think, "If I sleep with him, then he will know I care or love him. However making love to a person is one of many love languages but not the only way to express your heart for a person." But that's not always true. I know many people will disagree with me because I said "not always." But truthfully some men and women really believe that if you don't sleep with a person, you do not care about him or her. But that's not my argument. I recommend reading the Word of God to understand how Jesus designed the behavior of sex, fornication, and marriage and its process. I want you as a woman to know your worth, and you can't find it on your back or in whatever positions you prefer. Sex does not define you or your worth.

You discover your treasure in the face of God. You discover the true desire of your heart by submitting your inner feelings to the Lord. By doing so, knowing your value reveals you are a confident woman who knows what she wants, and it's not just sex and money. It's intimacy on many other levels, which includes caressing each other's minds and dreams. This includes a safe friendship, in which you trust the other with your fears, dreams, and insecurities in life, yes, even your weaknesses. But this is where most women get into disarray.

A woman might meet a guy she thinks is Mr. Right, and so she turns into Mrs. Right after one phone call and half a dinner. It's best to permit time for getting to know each other and to observe. I know this from my experiences. But this book is not titled How to Keep a Man: Volume 1. When my guy and I started to share time, conversations, and text messages, it meant a lot to me because I now had someone whom I could at least think about who brought a smile to my face and bubbly, butterfly feelings to my heart.

The real moment for me was when he saw my weakness, and it was OK because together we shared the same one and mirrored that back to each other. He said the most meaningful things to me, which settled me down when I found myself overwhelmed with emotions. But the moment of truth happened, even though we continued to stay in connection. I realized I was experiencing loneliness. My emotions were running rampant! But I told myself, "Don't expect, don't feel, try to relax, and just enjoy the ride." I felt like Princess Elsa in the animated Disney movie Frozen.

After a few months, it became much clearer to me: I liked him. But, ladies, you know what we do—some of us just want to confirm the status of the relationship. I didn't want to ask because my motto is "Just go with the flow." However, I found myself almost in pursuit mode for him. So I trained myself to back up and told myself, "Allow him to pursue you." Why was I behaving in such a manner? It's simple—I now had an emotional aspiration for him and was highly attracted to him. I had connected with him more deeply than I had revealed. I opened myself up to him when previously I had closed the door for friendship or any level of intimacy. But I found myself open to the point I wanted to talk to him daily. I definitely was interested in companionship.

So all these thoughts of "What's up with us?" were going through my mind because most men just will not come out and say what you want to hear when you think you should hear it. So here arises the inner turmoil of thinking, "He doesn't want to give me the truth," or "He's not feeling me," or "He has someone in another city," or "Maybe he's changed his mind and doesn't want to hurt me," or "Perhaps this is how he operates." I was clueless. But I knew how I felt. Why am I sharing this story with you? I'm telling you this because when you are alone or experiencing loneliness, if the right person shows up, you will encounter another form of loneliness if you feel that he or she is not where you are emotionally.

Let me remind you that I'm the strong woman whose mind was made up to continue being single for a while. I found myself having expectations for my relationship with him because he had said, "I'm here now. I'm not going any-where." Well, I took that as if it was "on and popping," as they say. But I was willing to walk away from a man who wasn't handling me like the treasure I am if I realized I was in this alone. I wasn't willing to chase behind a man; that wasn't my place. I wasn't going to force someone in my life or space if he didn't want to remain.

> *I had to remind myself, "I am the prize," and, yes, he might have called me the prize, but he didn't know that I was a gift with a hidden treasure. But I knew it. I was conscious, even if I would find myself alone or lonely, of not settling for being someone's pastime. His actions changed, and I paid attention. When I pay attention to people's actions, I am never fooled by their words. Actions don't lie. But sitting back and being observant teaches you that change is good. It helps you to learn a person's patterns and behaviors. And very subtle it reveals to you your acceptance, tolerance, and most importantly it teaches you your ability to give and receive love. It's amazing how you can't tell your heart to do what your mind is telling it. Especially when you've open your heart in an area that has been sealed. Today he's still the most amazing man in my life.*

A real woman is not waiting for a RICH man. She's preparing to be a wealthy wife. Spiritually and Financially

"One thing have I desired of the Lord, that will I seek after; that I may dwell in the house of the Lord all the days of my life, to behold the beauty of the Lord, and to inquire in his temple"

(Psalms 27:4).

Loneliness can be present at a time in your life when you don't desire companionship, while others may have someone presently in their life and yet struggle with feeling invisible. As the O'Jays song goes, "Your body is here with me, but your mind is on the other side of town." My dear sisters and brothers, some people live life in a box with a peephole for viewing beyond their absent reality, never removing the lid and never stepping out to pursue life beyond the last experience of heartbreak or rejection. A life lived in a shelter of solitude is a life not lived. But a life lived out of solitude is a life worth witnessing.

Many people think being alone is when you're by yourself, but what really makes you alone is being surrounded by the wrong people.

As a younger child, I found myself living life in a box with a peephole only for viewing. No one could enter, I refused to exit, and I permitted very few people to peep in. What do I mean by that? I was accustomed to living life behind a facade, yielding to no one the opportunity to get to know me or my true feelings, for many reasons: (1) I did not want anyone close to me, (2) I didn't know myself, and (3) I had made a conscious decision within to avoid verbally or

emotionally connecting with others only because I didn't want to expose my hurt or be hurt again. I only wanted people to see me from the outside, and sadly, I really didn't want people to see me, period. Why? It was because I was so broken and wounded.

I never allowed anyone in my personal, confidential sanctuary. If people were to see my pain, I would no longer appear to be the strong young lady they admired. So, very easily, I went through life doing what some do in the church—I unknowingly became a pretender. I pretended to be happy, pretended to feel whole. I did it. Why? Because sometimes that's what we birth, create, and produce in the walls of a religious sector called church. Some people choose to cover up their pasts, wounds, struggles, and weaknesses and what is needed are real testimonials of admitting setbacks and overcoming them.

My past is so ugly and so dark that the thought of my childhood drove me to attempt suicide while in the church arena. My life was so broken because people saw my sins and could not see my shame. How could I live in a world that condemned my sins and did not see my disgrace? People told me to come to Christ, but I did not see them measuring up to his character by giving love beyond what they deemed perfect. I was lost.

Scars from the Past

By the age of nine, I had been molested. By age twelve, I was raped by my older brother's friend. For years I never told a soul about either violation. Because my father was a pastor of the church, I kept the secrets, shame, torment, and false guilt within myself. I went through life as a little girl, damaged mentally and emotionally, and no one took the time to ask me what was wrong. No one noticed that my behavior had changed. No one noticed my head hanging, my rebellious conduct, or my outward show of anger and violence.

The people in the church just labeled me a "fast tail" little girl and "bad" preacher's daughter. They were more interested in my talent for singing for their own selfish purposes than in discerning my behavior to train me in my gift and calling. They missed it, like a lot of churches did and sometimes still do today. No one heard the scream of help beyond my ability to sing in the adult state choir, as if nothing had happened to me. Not one anointed person could see the deep depression I carried. As a child in the church, I was taught how to not show pain but to pretend as if I had it all together. Sadly and most often, many of the things we learn in our childhood will bleed over into adulthood, whether good or bad. However, the saints in the church sought my gift when Jesus wanted my soul. The church preferred a good sound of praise, which was to represent freedom, but never took the time to offer deliverance or healing through love.

The only thing I heard was, "You must be saved, and if you commit a 'sin,' then you are bound to hell.

A person who lives a life of Self-conviction is a person who doesn't believe there is no condemnation to them that are in Christ Jesus.

" If you had sex or committed fornication, you were guilty of the greatest sin. I felt like an outcast.

Not only had I been raped, but I also found myself without a place of restoration. I believed and felt the church had failed at compassion and the love walk. We are so quick to judge people by their actions before we open our hearts to just merely love them. We can be so quick to judge the skirt of a woman but not what she is really exposing—her lack of self-worth. We sometimes forget to take the time to be an ear before we condemn, as if that's what Jesus did. We make it so easy to shout over brokenness and wounds while we have churchgoing people who want to be free.

We need people to tell the truth and be transparent as to how they have risen above life's greatest pains. Few will tell you how they survived being a victim of rape, molestation, or physical or mental abuse. So when people like me go to church, they don't see themselves because other religious church folks are still pretending. In my entire childhood, I never heard anyone talk about these issues, so I felt like an outsider, which caused me to settle as a child into adulthood.

The worst part of holding on to memories is not the pain but the loneliness.

Until you are healed, you might have a tendency to make choices out of pain instead of wholeness. You might settle for less than you deserve. Because of my past, I made choices in relationships that brought me pain and scars, mentally and physically. I encountered physical abuse from men due to the fact that I didn't love myself enough because of the hand life dealt me. I wanted to be loved by someone so much that at age sixteen, I dated a boy who I thought really cared for me. I ended up pregnant, and because of the church, my pastoral parents, and a lot of pressure, I made a decision to have an abortion secretly. I just could not go through the embarrassment of being the preacher's daughter and pregnant. I had witnessed in the church how they treated sinners.

I witnessed young girls standing in front of the church to openly acknowledge they had fornicated and wanted to repent. I just did not want to go through the humiliation of it all, so I did what I thought was best at the time. Because of the lifestyle I was living, I wound up pregnant again at seventeen, and I had my son at eighteen. I thought I was single-handedly destroying my life and that God definitely did not love such a person as me. The result was that I felt, without a doubt, that it was time to love myself and my child.

When my parents found out I was pregnant, they put me out of the house but eventually allowed me to come back. To now enter into wholeness is a beautiful area to live in, beyond the pain of past hurts of a teenager in church or a present divorce—there's beauty in the ashes. The only way to overcome loneliness is to become self-assured.

Become your own celebration team. The day your soul opens up is the day the real you stands up and lives. You must not live life based on who's in it or who believes in you. Don't even create a space for people who choose not to celebrate you.

A person who has outlived the adversity

in his or her life

Will

outlive the opposition

of pain.

A person who outlives the adversity in his or her life is freed from the grip of pain. Live your life on purpose, and make it beautiful. If something or someone shows up that doesn't fit the puzzle, you will quickly recognize it because you've already made it your own masterpiece. After this, live.

TIP 5

※

Don't Settle

(It's Self-Sabotage)

When you settle, it's like standing at the seashore of the ocean waiting for a Bus to arrive.

SETTLE: TO SIN *k gradually or to the bottom, to be content with*

In 2012 The Daily Beast published an article titled "Why Men Are Settling for Mrs. Good enough." This article was a shock to me as it relates to statistics and the mind-sets of men and women. I'm very sure many will be in awe of the belief that many men are willing to settle for someone they are not in love with as long as she has all other attributes. The majority of people in today's society, as a distinctive group of single men and women, are under the debasing notion that women are the only ones willing to settle in relationships. Granted, I have heard many women make simpleminded statements, such as, "I'd rather have a piece of a man than no man at all." I find it unjust, immoral, and excessive that a mature and wise woman would dare to say or even permit this form of declaration to come out of her mouth. More or less, she's subjecting to or settling for a piece of anything borderline, "half a man." Why not just wait for what you desire and deserve?

It's frightening to me to believe that any self-secure, confident woman of internal wealth, with pride, dignity, and self-assurance, would desire someone other than who's best for her in her life. Declarations and assertions like these, I believe, have blinded true men or potential husbands to prematurely misjudge women as a whole. It's amazing how many people in our African American culture believe, or even agree with, the sad stigma that our black women are the least likely to fall in love with men they believe are their hearts' desire.

The moment you start to settle for less than what you deserve, you will end up with less than what you settle for

Part of this enlightening article, published February 2012, by reporter Jessica Bennett is reprinted here:

[Anthropologist Helen] Fisher's study unearthed some startling tidbits about sex, romance, and hooking up among the 6,000 men and women surveyed: among them, that Republicans, apparently, have more orgasms; that gay men are more romantic; and ambitious women turn men on. But the biggest surprise? Certain gender roles appear to have flipped since the days of The Rules and He's Just Not that Into You.

Men reported that they fell in love just as often as women, were just as likely to believe that marriage is "forever," and scarcely bit when asked whether they'd prefer to "just date a lot of people." But most shocking was how many of the single men wanted to settle down—and how willing they were to lower their standards to make that happen.

When reading and digesting this article, as a single black woman, my mouth dropped. Below is the most discussed question among women, whether middle class or lower class and regardless of race or creed. For the most part, *it is underestimated conversation. Many women would stop in their tracks to add their opinions if the topic were brought up in a busy room full of independent, energetic women with hormones and menstrual cycles. It is the thought of many and the silent question of most single women: "Where are all the good men?"*

Here is more of Ms. Bennett's The Daily Beast article:

A 31 percent of adult men said they'd commit to a person they were not in love with—as long as she had all the other attributes they were looking for in a mate—and 21 percent said they'd commit under those same circumstances to somebody they weren't sexually attracted to. The equivalent numbers for women were far lower.

"Give me a friend I get along with, have good sex with, and is willing to compromise, and I'll build the love over time," one man, a Colorado computer instructor, told me.

This man was in his forties. The percentage of men saying yes to imperfect commitment was actually highest among men in their twenties, almost 40 percent of whom said they'd commit without love (compared with 22 percent of women). The gap narrowed as men and women entered their thirties and widened again past forty. Yet regardless of age, men's willingness to answer in the affirmative to both questions was significantly higher across the board.

"Don't settle." Numerous people tell themselves these words after a breakup, after a mutual split, or, for a better term, after things have fallen apart or gone sour. The fact remains that a part of a person feels as if he or she deserved better than what he or she settled for or received. The most silent, unpredictable, and uncertain time in your life is when you decide to move on from your past. I admonish every person to do a self-inventory of you prior. Many times, when coming out of an experience that caused some sort of pain, if you are not wise and healed, you might unconsciously but willingly choose another relationship that's not ideal for you.

49

When you settle your Someone Extremely Terrified to Led Effectively.

If you are not completely restored to health emotionally, you might find comfort serenading in the wind for a temporary fix, which only presents momentary agony for a split second versus an eternal partnership and a fully developed capacity for a sacred eternal love with a lifetime mate. Why settle for convenience when covenant is waiting? We allow ourselves to go through the motion of just having attention or a fleeting moment of joy. It's challenging to be by yourself when everything in you desires a family, a spouse, and a companionship. It's an awakening moment when you want someone to talk to or have had a great day and would like to share that with someone. The aggravating yet lovely reality can be jarring when no one is there to share it with.

I know all my born-again, Holy Ghost–filled, saved readers are disagreeing with me because you know the truth that "God is always with us." That is true. However, I must keep it totally one hundred. God is with you and me and everyone, but there are times when some would like companionship or friendship from the opposite gender—not necessarily another marriage, boyfriend, or sex, at the moment but a person to spend time with, to share a movie with, to laugh with without the pressure of wondering, "Where is this going?" This is just my opinion on the subject. (Please send all controversial comments to my e-mail…lol.)

Believe it or not, saved single women and men still desire sex and companionship, and if the truth were told, many struggle in the area of fornication because they can't find a mate because of the religious talk regarding dating in the church (another topic for another book). However, friends and family can say they are going to walk through this divorce or heartbreak process with you, but there comes a point in this journey when you just have to walk this road unaccompanied. You will cry, and you will wish for someone to console you, and there's nothing wrong with that.

You just need to know the new you before you allow someone else to enter your new life. You must single-handedly deal with and destroy these seeds of divorce, murder, sabotage, and fear by uprooting and denouncing it to continue to germinate in your bloodline.

The only difference in who you are now and who you want to be and what you desire to accomplish depends on how many times you settle.

Bennett's Daily Beast article points out the following:

Fisher, a research professor at Rutgers University, explains it this way. "We have a stereotype in this culture that it's men who are the ones who don't want to commit, who don't want to settle down, who are the scarce resources. But in fact, it's the opposite."

When I went over this topic with some of my male friends and associates, 90 percent of fifty men agreed with Fisher's research. The majority of these men I knew and others had been invited to this private forum, so I was in total disbelief at the statistics that unfolded. The unrevealed truth stood in the room as a pink elephant. It was awkward, and it was the topic of discussion for hours. One friend said he'd rather have a faithful woman who was a good mother and hard worker versus her being good in the bedroom. And, of course, the debate was on.

Some men felt that sex and money were the most important factors but would settle for the money and OK sex. To my surprise, the majority agreed that physical attraction was important but that a woman didn't have to be a supermodel. Yet, within the confines of the statement all agreed she had to be willing to submit and have sex on a weekly basis, as well as not be needy.

As I breathed in the moment, I remained composed and in a tranquil posture and passionate regard of what men want. From a sista's observation, I said to all fifty of them, "Beauty is acceptable, but please look beyond the beauty and shapely figure to see if she has a prayer life, her own mind, and knows who she is before you make her wife material." I had a sincere dialogue, I observed, and I listened to the candid, very forward, and sometimes comical but, most important, heartfelt men in the room. I felt as if I were in the lion's den. They became predators, and I was the prey, figuratively speaking.

I had never seen so much testosterone in one room flaring as if they were being made to agree with one another. And, hilariously speaking, they didn't have to. It is amazing how people view their opinions as factual when they are simply beliefs or convictions. However, it was shocking, yet an awesome eye-opener, to observe, in a room of men in their twenties through fifties, how eager and desiring they were for companionship. And, of course, there were those I labeled the ants in the room—an ant is not big enough to carry his own weight but desires women to take care of him. Nevertheless, of course, at his thirty years of prime intelligence, he was put on mute by the only woman in the room—me.

A smart woman never says all that she knows and never reveals all that she has. She's Sharpe enough

to stand with silent power and speak as gentle as a two edged sword.

Astonishingly, in an awkward twist, the beautiful truth is that all these brilliant black men are educated and financially stable; some were divorced, some had never been married, and some were with or without children. And the most shocking and only agreeable question and conversational piece was when they all finally agreed on one question: "Where are all the good women?" This blew me away! My jaw dropped!

As a single, educated black woman with a lot of beautiful attributes going for myself—and the only woman in the room—I felt compelled and obligated to stand and speak up for my sisters by saying, "Here I am!" Conversely, I lightheartedly shared with them that there were as many women out there waiting as there were men who are looking for them. I said to them, as I would say to my sisters, **"Don't look for someone to complete you—look for the person who will accept you completely."**

I told them, "For myself, I desire to have someone who will accept me completely, being a mother, a minster, and a businesswoman. I want a man who will love me beyond my 'titles.' But when I fall, or in some cases commit a 'sin,' because he knows I love God, I'm not judged by my fall but loved for my transparency to admit I'm not perfect and yet still serving and thirsting for more of God."

But the question remains for so many single people: How are they missing one another? The truth is many are in a relationship where they are presently settling because they don't want to be alone. Some are involved in the dating process with a person who will never commit, and they prayerfully believe he or she will be the person to change his or her mind. There are also those like myself—you're just realizing you would like to try this so-called fixation called dating, but you are knowingly and purposely still carrying yourself as if you're still taken or in a relationship. So you rarely get approached. And when some-one does show interest by approaching you, you choose not to act on it. And so you fulfill your life with family, careers, and goals. I'm not saying this is right or wrong. However, what I'm suggesting and have merely observed is this: You will know when you are ready to date or settle down. You can feel it within, but somewhere along the way, you have become so comfortable and content to being busy in your life. You might not know how to just slow down to even include someone in your space or personal sanctuary.

Yes, you can feel and sense it's time, and truly in your heart you want to, you might have even met someone or have talked to your friends regarding it, but the problem is you don't know how to go about it. So you continue about your business as usual. And, eventually, you will meet someone, and you find an interest in him or her and will not know how to just be with someone to connect emotionally or to get to know him or her beyond the outward person. So life continues on, and that person will just keep moving on. Honestly for myself, I don't want my life to be so busy that I miss out on the divine opportunity of a life of love and companionship.

Love can't always be measured by how long you wait. It is about how well you understand why you're waiting.

The Truth

I was having a great, productive day, and everything was falling into place. My businesses were thriving and enormously growing at a rapid pace. Unusual doors of opportunity were opening for me in the line of economic development, and ministry was life changing and fulfilling. My children were excelling and healthy. I was a very proud mother and happy woman.

All of a sudden, I wanted to just talk to someone, but no one was there for me to talk to. I really felt as if I wanted someone to help me celebrate life and all the new endeavors that were succeeding in my life, but, in actuality, I didn't need anyone there. It wasn't about celebrating—it was about filling the void, the emptiness. I hadn't realized the void existed and was very prevalent.

I did not desire to hear someone say, "It's going to get better." I already knew that. I didn't wish for someone to help me move past this moment. I needed this present moment to aid me in moving onward. I can truly testify that I had several moments of feeling alone, depressed, sad, and heartbroken. But, thanks to God and to my willing determination to be healed and whole, I took those moments and faced them. I wanted to be a better person, to fulfill my purpose on the earth for my children and for the next king God planned to bring me.

I made up my mind I would not allow anyone into my life until I was able to be with me, love me, and complete me. I spent quality time with myself. I learned new things about myself, what I enjoy, and took time to just get to know Melissa (a.k.a. Mel). I'm so pleased and appreciative that I did. Now, I'm OK with celebrating my life's accomplishments all by myself. Now in my life, I'm not frustrated being single. I'm happy, whole, and waiting.

"Brethren, I count not myself to have apprehended: but this one thing I do, forgetting those things which are behind, and reaching forth unto those things which are before" (Philippians 3:13 KJV).

Occasionally, you just have to face the pink elephant in the room that has a lot of questions: How do I move past this? How do I deal with this without settling or cheating myself? You settle for what your pain portrays as a permanent failure until you make a decision to grow from this displacement. You can conquer, face, and come to grips with any challenge: "This is a hurdle in my life that only I can leap over."

Through the hurt and joy you will survive, but you must discover this by living it out. You will understand the strength you have once you feel and rise above your weakest point. You will know the greatness in you when you break free of mediocrity. Don't allow your present state to derail you from a precious road of intimate exposure, hidden desires, and the pleasure of following God's timing. Poet Maya Angelo said, "Do the best you can until you know better. Then when you know better, do better."

The most enormously popular quote from Polonius in William Shakespeare's Hamlet states, "To thine own self be true." This famous and legendary saying is often spoken yet is rarely lived when it comes to relationships. This season in your life is not a setback but a setup you've been waiting for all your life. If you pay attention to the digital clock on the wall, you'll miss the most rewarding time of your life. A digital clock or time clock of our body is not worth your attention. I've heard many women say, "My biological clock is ticking." My suggestion is to remove the batteries and tap into the timing and rhythm of God.

Help Me!

There is a kairos moment that will happen in each one of our lives. This is a sequential time, an indeterminate moment when everything happens right before your eyes. If you are sensitive to the Holy Spirit, He will expand your discernment to recognize the dos and don'ts in this season of your life so you will understand the purpose for your life. Dr. Myles Munroe, a pastor, wrote in the book The Principles and Power of Vision that "[a] successful person is someone who understands, submits to, and adheres to the principles that will carry him or her to success." In other words, take this time to learn and acknowledge how you ended where you are now and follow the principles to move into success.

You must have a clear vision, and oftentimes a great fall can give you a clear vision. Use mistakes as lessons learned, and you will ultimately groom and advance your ability to achieve greater expansion in love and life—not because you had a fall, but because you got up and tried it again. You will become a person who must rest in an awaiting posture for God's direction and purpose for your life.

Clear direction will be visible when you're able to focus beyond a broken heart or a broken sprit, a cluttered mind filled with dangerous emotions and thoughts and I wishes. What is in touchable reach and visible with a whole heart is stated in Proverbs 20:5 (ESV): "The purpose in a man's heart is like deep water, but a man of understanding will draw it out." In other words, we all have a vision, whether happily married or frustrated and divorced.

One's vision causes that dream and purpose to be brought out so it can become reality. Disconnect from what has been disconnecting you from your purpose in life or your inner waters and your godly desires will flow as you understand the depth of your being. You have the capacity to dive deeper into the purpose of God for your life. This is His only desire for you. When you're just crying because "it's over," God does not consider this a broken spirit. I know that, for me as a Christian, I wanted to make this time in my life deep and all that God is taking me through. When in actuality I was about what He wanted to reveal to me about myself, choices, and even the root of why I am who I am at this point in my life. But it's not. This is not the moment when God is telling you to be Jonah and go to Nineveh. Not! Nope! He's telling you to pour yourself at his feet so He can lead, heal, and restore you.

Jonah's fear and pride cause him to run from God. He didn't want to go to Nineveh to preach repentance to the people, as God has commanded, because he felt they were his enemies, and he is convinced that God will not carry out his threat to destroy the city. Instead, he boards a ship for Tarshish, which is in the opposite direction of where God had told him to go. Soon a raging storm causes the crew to cast lots and determine that Jonah is the problem. They throw him overboard, and he is swallowed by a great fish. In its belly for three days and three nights, Jonah repents his sin to God, and the fish vomits him up on dry land (we wonder what took him so long to repent). Like many of us, sometimes we have to experience a situation to bring us back to a place of purpose.

We cannot hide from God. What He wishes to accomplish through us will come to pass, despite all our objections and foot dragging or being divorce or single. However, this is the moment for self-evaluation. This is not the time to move on to the next assignment in your life and push this moment under a rug. God was getting Jonah's attention because He wanted Jonah to fulfill an assignment as does He with you, but it starts with surrendering not running from this moment in your life.

Ephesians 2:10 reminds us that He has plans for us and will see to it that we conform to those plans. How much easier it would be if we, unlike Jonah, would submit to Him without delay!

This is the very place some run from, but it's the position and that place of refurbishing that are so urgently needed. Uncertainty about life is not so easily entertained, talked about, or exposed, yet your soul reaches forth in faith of the unknown, where your heart that's bleeding can get the electric shock wave of a lifetime. It's OK to scream, yell, and curse and to let the snot roll and mascara run! For once, it's OK to break the silence and just be you, whoever you are. It's OK to not have all the answers. It's even OK not to be there for anyone else but you right now in this moment. David said in Psalm 109:26 (NIV), "Help me, Lord my God; save me according to your unfailing love." What was David, the "friend of God," saying in this vulnerable state?

David, from a perceived hole in his soul, was projecting an outward spilling of emotions. He was unraveling the inner sound of a sacred truth that many others close to him did not see, recognize, or care about. David said, "Help me!" This gut-wrenching sore from within ushered David to a place of desperation. Have you ever been in a place of desperation? Where it no longer mattered who saw you with your hands lifted at the altar? Where it was no longer a concern with whom you shared the same heartbreak story again and again?

Have you ever been in such desperate despair that you actually considered returning to the same person or situation that yielded pain to you because, in some strange way, that was the only place familiar to you? David the psalmist said, "Help me!" My sisters and brothers, you must get to a place of acknowledging you need help. It's not always possible to receive healing or aid from the person who brought you pain. Regret for leaving a painful situation that was not healthy for you will not serve you. It's false evidence portraying reality.

In Psalm 63:1 (NIV), we find David saying, "My God, earnestly I seek you… my whole being longs for you." We all will face a season of great heartache and anticipation of healing for our soul. Referring back to Psalm 109, David says, "Help me, Lord my God; save me according to your unfailing love."

David knew the Lord loved him regardless. David had many things others can attest to doing in our their lives today that which they are ashamed to admit they did. But after all the sins he committed, David knew that "it didn't matter—God loves me."

David's prayer request is offered in Psalm 27:4 (KJV): "One thing have I desired of the Lord, that will I seek after; that I may dwell in the house of the Lord all the days of my life, to behold the beauty of the Lord, and to inquire in His temple." David found the heart of God through reaching for it. He brushed against the presence of God because he had no one else there to lay his face on, no one to whom he could disclose his weakness or sins. There was no one he felt would not judge his vulnerability or self-acclaimed shelter of safety. He found himself positioned on the seemingly open floor and lay prostrate, alone, not because his wife wasn't accessible or because he was a king with rulers and maids and people who admired him at his beck and call. No.

David cried out to God because he needed a savior. He needed more than what some physical person could give or introduce. He craved, begged, pursued, grabbed, and longed for a simple, mere touch from God. He didn't need words; he didn't require a monetary blessing; he didn't call for another concubine; he didn't yearn for more children or materialistic items. He needed the safety of his Father's hand extending an open reach and securing the grip of his son's fingers. God embraces and holds the surrender of the hand of a broken son, the fragile yet strong muscle of the heart that gives life and takes it away.

That one vessel, the heart, can inspire the hardest, tough guy in the room to cry and the softest woman to not shed a tear. This muscular organ can pump blood through the veins, in one moment giving life and in the next moment stopping. It is when the heart stops or malfunctions that physical life discontinues. David wasn't concerned about the natural functioning of the heart but about its drive in making vital decisions. The heart does not drive your decisions but instead responds to the choices you make. David desired the desirable and wasn't going to let go until he obtained it.

You don't need another man, woman, business deal, ideal investor, or another client; you need what David longed for—not just a one-night stand or quick rendezvous, but a consistent experience that is set apart from all other life-changing chronicles ever imagined, dreamed, or lived. David went back to that same place often, because once true authentic love is encountered, nothing and no one can compare. David wanted an irremovable seed to be sown and planted in his heart and soul, and only God, the wisest gardener, could plant a seed of such depth and riches.

David reached a place of safety and security in God. He surrendered his whole heart and soul to a God whom he knew loved him no matter what he did or had done. How did David get there? He was transparent with his very heart to God. And so should you. You will reach the climax of your soul when you step away from the shadow of your pain. You must come from the darkest place, beyond the outward, external surface, to the brightest but sacred altar that reveals the ultimate path of freedom in exposed light, life, and breath.

Say, "This is it. I surrender all." Trust Him to love you like David—"according to His unfailing love." That's the love you really long for. Embrace the "David attitude" with a thug tone and an arch in your back and say, "He still loves me, yeah!" And pat yourself on the chest because He does. That's when you get clear direction. If you are awaiting the truth to be revealed, it starts with your being truthful and honest with yourself regarding what's in your heart. *Jeremiah 17:9–10 (NIV) says,* **"The heart is deceitful above all things and beyond cure. Who can understand it?** *I the Lord search the heart and examine the mind."*

The heart is hopelessly dark and deceitful, a puzzle few can figure out. God gets to the heart of the human, to the root of things. He treats them as *they really are, not as they pretend to be.*

Please, don't settle.

It is better to believe an obvious lie

than to swallow a deceitful truth.

—Dennis E. Adonis

TIP 6

❧

Rejection—Deal with It

REJECTION IS THE *shunning of a person's affection; to refuse to accept, or to deny, or to acknowledge or discard as useless; to discard or throw away and to isolate.*

Marriage, also called matrimony, tying the knot, or wedlock, is a socially or ritually recognized union by which two individuals make their relationship public and permanent. There are so many books regarding marriage nowadays that it simply sends a red flag that the enemy has launched a poisonous and lethal attack on marriages that in turn destroys the family. In truth marriage is not just an example for the children in your families or generation—it is the prime example, model, and structure for the body of Christ, which is the church. The marriage between husband and wife is a shining light that eliminates ungodly illusions and images of marriage or covenant.

It is amazing how times have changed. Statistically and culturally, when one speaks about marriage, it sometimes sounds like a foreign word being taught to people who are hearing this utterance *for the first time. But how do you deal with overcoming rejection from a previous marriage or relationship? Some people can't possibly understand how one can be rejected in marriage or any form of intimate relationship. But it happens all the time. Many spouses deal with rejection from the other, the one they love. The trouble or danger about love is it has no boundaries. So when dealing with rejection from a previous mate, you ask yourself, "How did I permit this to happen?" The truth is that when love has no boundaries, you freely open yourself with the thought they would never hurt you, or push you away. Rejection never enters your mind.*

Love is like a loud, silent earthquake that pulls all the corners of your soul to-gether to create a huge, shattering shake within your emotions to quickly change your concept about love and all its phases.

Love is known to have many faces. It creates an avenue for joyous moments while turning away from love becomes the breeding ground for rejection and a host of emotional stages. Love within a marriage, a family, or even a platonic friendship has the ability to breathe life, one of the most powerful tools a person has. Love escorts an individual to his or her grave without a pronouncement of death by a physician or an in-hand death certificate if a person is not loved Godly and wisely. Love should not be the death of your soul, but love should give an everlasting life of serenity and joy. Love has a funny way of revealing its highs and lows. One person's perceived lack of love from one incident can cause mass destruction in a home, a community, or a business. Many emotions such as rejection, aggression, and anger are bullets for people who don't yet fully identify that what they experience in life stems from love or its seeming lack, even in marriage.

In 2001, the US Surgeon General issued a report stating that rejection was a greater risk for adolescent violence than drugs, poverty, or gang member-ship. Countless studies have demonstrated that even mild rejection leads people to take out their aggression on innocent bystanders. School shootings, violence against women, and fired workers going postal are other examples of the strong link between rejection and aggression. However, much of that aggression elic-ited by rejection is also turned inward.

Sadly, we now live in a world where teen violence is viewed as the new social-media reality show. In the city where I reside, a group of African American teenage girls were in a verbal dispute on Facebook. This outraged anger went "princess gangsta" in a matter of conversations between the teenagers on social media. They all decided to meet at a local park to face one another and fight in front of a crowd of witnesses, including adults, while video recording the new "Parks" boxing match to publicize on social media. Regrettably, one fourteen-year-old girl was shot and killed and two other teen girls were shot and in-jured when a boyfriend got involved. This was a senseless murder. Within the same week, another fourteen-year-old, a black male, was gunned down while walking home from the library and ran to die on his grandmother's porch. Reportedly his death had to do with a previous altercation with a teen girl. Her boyfriend and his friend shot and killed this young African American child.

Why am I sharing such heartfelt and tragic stories? Because somewhere in the hearts and minds of these individuals was a gap or mental breakdown in distinguishing love versus anger, love versus hate, love versus rejection. At the end of the storyline, devastation revealed what unresolved emotions can generate and bring into being—murder. Whether physical or mental, rejection can kill the human soul.

Every time you think you are being rejected from something good, it's actually God redirecting you to something better.

The Scarlet Letter

We often hear people use the term rejection. Many couples reference this term, stating that a mate rejects them. But the funny part of the term is the other person never seems to own his or her role or admit the directed emotion is true, at least to the person who feels it. I'm reminded of a dramatic love story titled The Scarlet Letter.

The Scarlet Letter is an 1850 romantic work of fiction in a historical setting, written by Nathaniel Hawthorne, and is considered his magnum composition of literal art. Set in Puritan Boston, Massachusetts, between 1642 and 1649, it tells the story of Hester Prynne, who conceives a daughter through an affair. With great effort to create a new life of repentance and self-respect, she is portrayed as a woman condemned by her Puritan neighbors. Throughout the book, Hawthorne explores themes of legalism, sin, and guilt and rejection.

Hester is sent to the New World by her husband, who later assumes the name of Roger Chillingworth, as he has some business to finish before he can join her back in Boston. After he is shipwrecked and captured by Native Americans and presumed dead, Hester continues to live her life as a seamstress in the town. She looks to the local pastor Arthur Dimmesdale for comfort; somewhere along the way, passion between them emerges, culminating in the conception and subsequent birth of their child, Pearl. Because Hester has no husband with her, she is imprisoned, convicted of the crime of adultery, and sentenced to be forced to wear a prominent scarlet letter A for adultery for the rest of her life.

For Hester, the scarlet letter is a manifestation of her sin and a reminder of her painful solitude. She contemplates casting it off to obtain her freedom from an oppressive society and a scarred past, as well as an absence of God. Because the society excludes her, she considers the possibility that many traditions held up by the Christian Puritan culture are untrue and are not designed to bring her happiness.

Because they reject her, Hester spends her life mostly in solitude or isolation. To me The Scarlet Letter reveals her strength, courage and perseverance yet a silent trinity: rejection, loneliness, and solitude. Many have encountered or experienced what supermodels call a runway experience, by which the only designer attire you wear is a prominent scarlet letter R for rejection. It is on a silent display, but the only one who feels it is you, particularly during a season of life when experiencing a divorce or other form of heartbreak.

In many families or friendships, we've known someone who had to deal with this silent torment called rejection. Many people have had to deal with this silent affliction, which seems to destroy our identity or sabotage our very own purpose in life. Many of us have not only had to live through rejection but have also felt the need to act as if it was not present or didn't happen. We've had to *pretend as if it weren't real, as if we were OK, and as if the person or people inflicting such a feeling among us didn't mean it the way we heard it or the way it really made us feel.*

Most people, women and many men, will tell you that in a divorce, the feeling of rejection is the first present emotion that arises. But it's often a familiar feeling—whether it was a job you applied for and were denied the position; or maybe a spouse you felt tolerated you and not celebrated you; or perhaps Mom or Dad had his or her favorite, and it didn't matter what you did since little Shanika always got the praise, but your parent didn't realize you felt rejected. Just maybe, the other kids didn't pick you to count in the childhood game of hide-and-seek. From wherever these feelings originated, rejection has stuck its deceitful head up in all our lives when we least expected it.

Hester Prynne, in The Scarlet Letter, brings us hope in redefining life after rejection. For some people in marriage, rejection has hit you with a blow and knocked you to your knees. Or for someone serving God, it might appear as if the emotional investment is not going to pay off simply because you asked Him to keep your marriage together and it didn't last. It feels like no matter how many times you forgive, your heart still gets broken time and time again. For some, it seems that they've been waiting a long time for their prayers to be answered, while everybody else is getting the house, the husband, the business, and, yet, they stand faithfully, still waiting.

But that's in the world. How do you deal with rejection in the church? What happens when you come to the church broken and no one has time for you and they just want to know your business? Or the ones you open up to because you're so broken and they spread all your secrets? Why is it in some of our local assemblies many people are rejected by how they dress, or maybe their tattoos, better yet when someone doesn't look like the traditional believer? Why do the saints feel like the people in the world are more loyal? Hester and you have more in common than you know. That is my assignment in this book, through the anointing of God, is to "impregnate you with strength while conveying to you that your true identity can be birthed and obtained amid adversity, a failed marriage, and when fighting rejection.

God used me to write this book to help you redefine your purpose in life, to encourage you to get your positive focus back. After all the hurt, all the lawyers in the courtroom, all the blame, all the times of being misunderstood, all the bad choices, it's time to get your life back—as a single person. Hester, after being ostracized as the black sheep, decides to remain in the town where people know her. She stays on to hear and face what her neighbors have to say about her sin. That's what's going on with many of you—God allowing your enemies to witness your comeback or your reveal!

In forgiving, you don't just learn to just deal with rejection but also teach yourself not to practice tit for tat. There's no winner in that. If at some point you decide to move on, then let it all go, including what others said, how they did not support you, or even how they made you feel. One way to overcome is to discuss with someone how you felt about the rejection. You must be willing to trust someone, to release all the pain and disappointments without emotionally dumping on that person. Be open, sharing your true feeling so you won't hold him or her hostage. I admonish you to make sure it is someone who's trustworthy. Gather all the parts of you and put them back together. Reclaim any parts of you still attached to someone else.

Turn every no into a yes. The best way to move on and get over a breakup is to see you doing everything you never believed you could. Start your business, lose the weight, and go back to school. Remember that this is not to prove anything to anyone else—it's to prove to yourself that you are in control of your own life. To the townspeople who wanted to kill her spirit Hester not only proved that she is determined to stand through all the adversity. She stands and faces them, making a declaration that her strength will not waver in the wake of their rejection. Her confidence rises to the occasion when she decides to face those who know her past to show them that they could not dictate or stop her future. It's time to remove the scarlet letter from your chest and live beyond this moment.

When a person rejects you,

it doesn't mean you are not good enough.

It just reveals that he or she was too

insecure to walk with you.

What you think is their rejection is re-

ally Gods protection.

TIP 7

—⁓—

Command Your Day

COMMAND: *TO HAVE* authority or control over; to demand, to govern, to dominate as if from an elevated place

"Summing it all up, friends, I'd say you'll do best by filling your minds and meditating on the things true, noble, reputable, authentic, compelling, gracious—the best, not the worst; the beautiful, not the ugly; things to praise, not things to curse. Put into practice what you learned from me, what you heard and saw and realized. Do that, and God, who makes everything work together, will work you into his most excellent harmonies" (Philippians 4:8–9 MSG).

The most strategic, powerful, and rewarding days begin with rising early in the morning to seek the face of God to decree and declare what you expect and believe for your day. The Bible says in Matthew 6:11, "Give us this day our daily bread." Daily we receive fresh food or sustenance, directions, assurance, and comfort by seeking Him before the day starts. Whether or not you believe it, before your feet hit the floor, God has already planned something for you before the sun rises, and all you have to do is line up with His will. In 1 Peter 5:8 (KJV) it says, "Be sober, be vigilant; because your adversary the devil, as a roaring loin, walketh about, seeking whom he may devour." It is the mission of the adversary to distract you before you remember who you are in God, but it has no power over you as you consciously choose to step into your divine assignment on earth.

The Word says in Jeremiah 29:11, "For I know the plans I have for you,' declares the Lord, "plans to prosper you and not to harm you, plans to give you hope and a future."

Present your soul as an offering in the presence of an almighty God, not just on your behalf but also for those to whom you are connected. To rise early to worship Him, and whisper to Him how amazing He is and how much you love Him, is the legal access you have as a son or a daughter. For Him to talk to you as you dwell in His secret place is the most rewarding intimacy you could ever experience. Even if He doesn't say anything, knowing you exist before the King is a moment to cherish. To present and offer to God the first fruits of your day is a sure indication to God that your trust is in Him, even in a time of your life when you feel broken or confused about a relationship that has ended.

The Bible says in Proverbs 3:6 (KJV), "In all thy ways acknowledge Him and He shall direct thy path." Nothing can defeat, stop, or be withheld from a person who lives in the posture of surrender, worship, and prayer. It is my firm beliefs that as you walk with God, grow in God, and live in God, He will walk and live with you and adhere to everything that concerns you. This is a summons to every woman and man, in whatever stage of life, to recommit to a consistent life of prayer. I truly believe the most important relationship in our lives should be the one we are intimately the reciprocator of, and that is the lover of our souls, the Lord Jesus Christ. There is nothing like the presence of the Lord. I have come to know that there's absolutely nothing like having God be the foundation of your life. You can be open, broken, and transparent, and He remains loveable, touchable, reachable, forgivable, and merciful.

This book was birthed through a very trying and difficult time in my life, and in it, I give you ten tips to move forward and, yes, they all are great forerunners. But one of the most important tips is this one: "Command your day." Everything starts in Him and ends in Him. When you can command your day, your life is being positioned in divine alignment with God. When you let go of your own will by humbling yourself in prayer, you enter into a sequence in the heavens. You enter into the elements and rhythm of God.

As you begin to enter this new era of your life, please know that your words build the next chapter, the next business, the next relationship. The words you speak are the paintbrush swaying and creating on a temporarily blank canvas. It fills in a picture from scratch into a portrait. What you speak from *your heart by faith becomes the visible evidence of your declarations. When you decree and declare, what you are purposely speaking into the atmosphere is "I agree with God. I agree that I sit in heavenly places. I agree, so I decree that every generational curse is broken from my bloodline. I agree so I declare the brokenness of my soul is healed. I agree so I decree that my emotions are stable and sound." I agree that my children will not experience this form of heartbreak. I close every door, crack, or window that is open in my bloodline from my ancestors that will try to enter into the lives of my children and their children. I bind every and all illegal spirits and that will attempt to enter in my future and all those connected to me that will cause any form of insecurities, pride, selfishness, rejection, low self-esteem, and bondage and render them all helpless. I agree that I have victory and that God is my source of strength and resources. Agree that as I empty myself to the Lord, He will restore me and freely give me joy, peace, patience, and the ability to move forward as I live a healthy and whole life in Him.*

All these declarations are what you speak in agreement with the word of God in His presence and believe in faith that what you decree you shall have, according to Matthew 21:22, "And all things, whatsoever ye shall ask in prayer, believing, ye shall receive.

You have now created the title deed to your future. When you command your day, you ultimately enter into a place of rest. Matthew 18:18 (NIV) says, "Whatever you bind on earth will be bound in heaven, and whatever you loose on earth will be loosed in heaven."

When you operate in the authority given unto you by the Most High, you walk in the same power as the great "I AM." The Bible says in Acts 1:8 (NLT), "You will receive power when the Holy Spirit comes upon you." The power that is the authority of God takes the liberty to move beyond your natural ability into the supernatural and live in that which breaks all boundaries of the human mind and capability and knowing. The confines of your being must be subject to the Spirit of God. You must continually submit your human nature to the Father. And the most critical part is your mind, which houses and holds your memory. That memory of your being has to resurrect and ascend.

If your mind continues to execute according to its natural performance and design, it will constantly remind you of what was and not what shall be. It will ultimately lead you to a place of depression, regret, and death. In 2 Corinthians 10:5 (KJV) says, "Casting down imaginations, and every high thing that exalteth itself against the knowledge of God, and bringing into captivity every thought to the obedience of Christ."

If you demand your flesh to change its way of thinking, you will break the cycle of destruction and heartbreak. Otherwise, your life will not change, and you will continue to have the same experiences but with a different partner, that same downtrodden spirit drawn to another individual but with a different name. The Bible says in Romans 12:2 (NIV), "Do not conform to the pattern of this world, but be transformed by the renewing of our mind." If your mind is not transformed or renewed daily, you continue to operate in the lower dimension for your life. This could lead to poverty, settling to remain on a job when God has equipped you to be an entrepreneur, not identifying with your worth and identity and ultimately living an unfulfilled life. You will only have what the world permits versus what God promises already belong to you. His promises will manifest on this earth and in this lifetime through your decrees and obedience.

Merriam-Webster defines decree as "an official order given by a person in power or by a government; a religious ordinance enacted by council or titular head." This is such an awesomely clear illustration of who you are and the weight you carry in God according to what He has given you jurisdiction and authority over. The reason it is so important to live in the presence of God during this time of your life is because it is the desire of the enemy to sift you as wheat.

Luke 22:31–32 (NIV) says, "Simon, Simon, Satan has asked to sift all of you as wheat. But I have prayed for you, Simon, that your faith may not fail. And when you have turned back, strengthen your brothers."

The Message version of Luke 22:31–32 says, "Simon, stay on your toes. Satan has tried his best to separate all of you from me, like chaff from wheat. Simon, I've prayed for you in particular that you not give in or give out. When you have come through the time of testing, turn to your companions and give them a fresh start."

Wow, this scripture provides a clear picture as to how the plan of the enemy is to destroy you, whether through the wrong relationships, the wrong job, or the curse words you speak out of your mouth. And what better way to seize you than when you're in a place of brokenness of heart? When you are heartbroken or lonely is the time you're prone to feel tempted to allow unhealthy friends, desires, relationships, and thoughts that might influence you to abort the call of God on your life. It is during your most vulnerable seasons of your life when you feel as if life has dealt you the wrong hand. This is when it can be very tempting to lose sight of God's promises for you. That's why the Message version says, "Satan has tried his best to separate all of you from me." How so? Through your divorce, through the person you thought would be with you till "death do you part." It is in your heartbreak that you wrestle with dangerous emotions and struggle with thoughts of failure. It is at the root of the issue that you will struggle in your flesh, which is your will, mind, and negative emotions, and not just sexually. But some thoughts clearly go against the true promises of God according to His word for your life, which will birth healing and restoration. A person who is consistent in prayer will have conquered a major war within, finding internal peace before moving on to the next relationship. A person who is not in worship might try to fulfill the vacancy with a movie, a hot date, or some pleasurable enjoyment. Or if aligned with God's will, one could be guided to just the right movie that delivers an uplifting message or could have a friendly date with someone who is a blessing to meet. But that will not restore you and fix the situation. The Bible says in Luke 22:32 (Message) "I've prayed for you in particular that you not give in or give out."

Command not just early in the morning but throughout your day. You must be consistent to turn away from your flesh so you won't make foolish decisions or allow your emotions to lead you down a less desirable path. During this season of your life, it is most important to repent, forgive, and surrender your will. In commanding your day in prayer, you will find a new love for His presence. By commanding your day, I promise that this will be your new residence. When you move into the next chapter of your life, this will remain your starting place. Command your day—it is your best option.

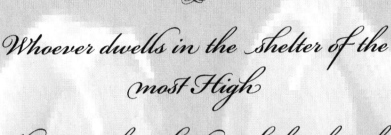

Whoever dwells in the shelter of the
most High

will rest in the shadow of the almighty.

I will say of the Lord,

"He is my refuge and my fortress,

my God, in whom I trust."

Psalms 91:1–2

(NIV)

TIP 8

It's Your Time to Shine

AND IF I ask you to name all the things that you love, how long would it take for you to name yourself?

There are so many reasons we deny ourselves the ambiance of truth. Sometimes it's simply because we have experienced so many setbacks or interruption that we feel stagnant. We've limited our expectations of the truth and certainty of our true existence and purpose in life. We feel it has limited our very reality and authenticity that we can live beyond pain and failures, such as going through a divorce or having a child out of wedlock or not finishing school or being fired from a job.

Yet, stand tall and hold your head up high even when you know the very family and friends you thought would have your back seemed to put a knife in it. Never to say, "I'm sorry." Regardless of whatever life-challenging moment has risen within the confounds of your being, whether male or female, the truth declares you are greater than the fall, wiser than the bad choice, and more successful than the toughest rejection.

Today it's time for you to shine! It's time for you to rise beyond what you allowed to snuff your light and now enter into a place of reflection. Let the reflection of your determination and strength shine as bright and beautiful as the rays of the sun. Look yourself in the mirror and declare, "It's my time to shine." Expect the best and know you deserve it. Make conscious decisions that there will not be a limit to what you can accomplish as long as you focus not on what once stopped you but on what's pushing you forward.

Start that business, write that book, and go back to school. Whatever you desired to do before your light went dim, it's time to dream again! You were born for this! Shine, my sisters and brothers! Shine and testify! Go forward in your life!

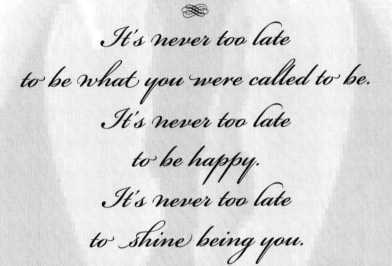

It's never too late
to be what you were called to be.
It's never too late
to be happy.
It's never too late
to shine being you.

TIP 9

❦

Move Forward

in Motivation

There is no better motivation than adversity. Every defeat, every heartbreak, every loss contains its own seed, its own lesson on how to improve your performance the next time.

—Malcolm X

MOTIVATION IS THE *desire to do things. It is your fight for focus for today that you do not want to put off for tomorrow. Motivation is your driving force to getting out of bed before dawn at 4:00 a.m. to fulfill your purpose. Your motivation is that inner "go get it," regardless of your attempting to do it without any training, simply because there is a driving force in you to make it happen. It's the essential component in conquering and setting goals—and research shows you can influence your own levels of motivation and self-control.*

Do not wait on someone to motivate you when you are the only inspiration you need. Your motivation should be your children, your surroundings, your bank account, and your personal view of your life as a whole. It becomes the heartbeat of your existence. And the only people who will understand your drive, your sleepless nights, your endless days, and your impulse to keep striving are other dreamers. The average or normal individual with a mediocre mind-set will not understand your motivation or drive because he or she needs a support team just to make a decision. You, on the other hand, have an internal green light that never turns red but sometimes turns yellow, and that's just to slow you down so you can catch your breath and view but not stop. However, your motivation should be balanced with rest and leisure activities. God is always found in moments of stillness. If you are not where you want to be in life, if where you are now is not appearing like the dream you had, or if where you see your life presently is not what or where God told you in your private prayer time, that should be enough motivation for you to "get up and go harder"!

The fact remains that if you continue to do what you have done previously, you will get the same results. Why expect anything different in life if you do not make the proper preparations to change things? If there was ever a time in your life to be your own cheerleader, that time is now. When your darkest days come, it is vitally important that you continue to know that God has a plan for your life.

Jeremiah 29:11 (NIV) says, "'For I know the plans I have for you,' declares the LORD, 'plans to prosper you and not to harm you, plans to give you hope and a future.'"

God has a plan and a promise for your life, and the enemy has a plan for your life as well. You just need to know which one to battle and which one to embrace. Everything that has taken place in your life to this point—every obstacle, heartache, joy, and accomplishment and every time you gave up, didn't finish what you started, felt letdown, and were set back—has a purpose. When it's all said and done, nothing will be wasted.

The Bible says in James 1:8 (KJV) "A double-minded man is unstable in all his ways." I say to you that the only way to keep yourself motivated is to make sure your mind is sound and stable. Correct your language and conversation. It should be in total, absolute agreement with what you believe. Your actions should display, as the old folks say, "down in your knowing" that this is what you want to accomplish. Sometimes this is what no sleep and long hours earn you, when God is calling you into a predestined time or preparing you for destiny promotion. This is what being consistent looks like. Who says a bad move can't achieve a good end? Double-talk brings double trouble. You determine the outcome of your movie. You have the ability and power to write the last scene of your life. But it's going to take your pushing yourself to get results. Push the boundaries of your so-called limitations—no one puts you there but you.

Break every chain, nullify and dismantle every word curse, and shut the door to negativity while you disconnect from dream killers. Motivation starts with you! It's your season! Get on it! What are you going to do? After this...

The most powerful action you will ever regret is to stop before you even start.

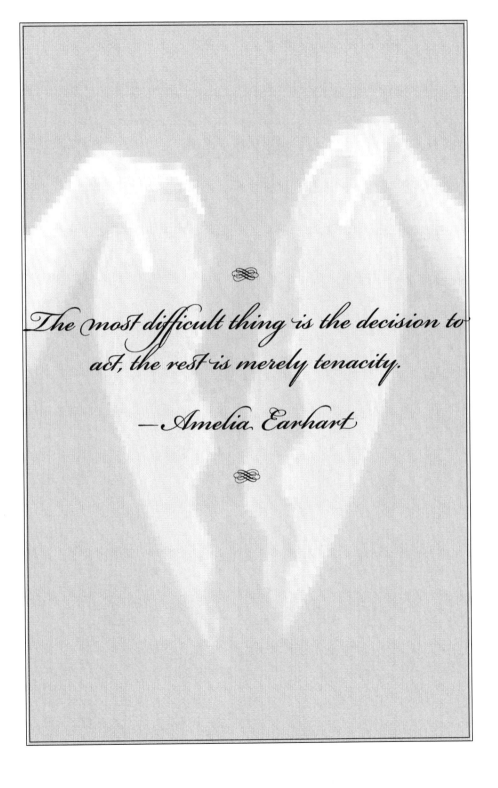

The most difficult thing is the decision to act, the rest is merely tenacity.

—Amelia Earhart

TIP 10

Love—Embrace the New You

You can never cross the ocean until you have the courage to lose sight of the shore.

—Christopher Columbus

EMBRACING THE NEW *you is an experience you can take pleasure in and from often. It's all about celebrating your uniqueness, the rise and growth of your significance. That includes embracing the ups and downs and permitting yourself to live a purposeful life. This entails unlocking, discovering, and uncovering the original and real you. The most amazing and ultimately life-changing encounter you will ever have is to discover is God's amazing, mind-blowing plan for your life, which you will discover is in some ways never-ending because of life's evolving cycles. An Arab proverb states that you should write the bad things that happen to you in the sand so that they can be easily erased from your memory. However, most of us engrave the bad things that happen to us in concrete; therefore, our painful memories remain immortalized in our minds. We walk around with our failures, our mistakes, our disappointments, and our hurts from the past shackled around our ankles, weighing us down.*

Behavioral expert Steve Maraboli in his book Unapologetically You: Reflections on Life and Human Experience quoted- "Renew, release, let go. Yesterday's gone. There's nothing you can do to bring it back. You can't 'should've' done something. You can only DO something. Renew yourself. Release that attachment. Today is a new day!

89

Sometimes letting go is simply changing the labels you place on an event while looking at the same event with fresh eyes. Unpack your suitcase! Take out everything, nicely folded and gently packed within your luggage that God has not designed or orchestrated for your journey. Unpack and let go of everything you were told about yourself that has made your life difficult, challenging, religious, and cluttered. Remove everything and anyone you desired and invited into your life that God has not orchestrated for your purpose and destiny. It is easier to embrace and accept who you are today in your own skin. You must embrace the real truth about you. You may be surprised by how many people's opinions you've allowed to live in you. How many people are walking in your shoes with you? You have not become a shadow of them. You've become an imitation of them. How many other people's personalities and ways have you unknowingly gravitated to, unaware of the influence they've had over your life? You might mimic how they speak, how they dress, how they perform, or how they choose to raise their children. This is easy to do when you are searching for guidance, longing for validation, and looking for approval. It's effortless to do when you are unfamiliar with how a particular task or venture should be done. And nothing is wrong with having a mentor or pastor or another person to guide you, but we should still be able to identify our true selves. Still be you. It's possible that in some people's lives, the real people, the essence of who they are, have not been able to shine because so many identities are being revealed and lived through them. Many people wonder through life trying to figure out who they are and what's there purpose in the earth. But you can't find out because you're not lost. You discover who you are by living life and seeking the will of God. You can never know who you are based solely on what someone tells you about who you are. Most people think they discover who they are by what they have a passion for and what they are gifted to do. Colossians 1:16 says "for everything, absolutely everything, above and below, visible and invisible… everything got started in him and finds its purpose in him. The purpose of your life is far greater than your own personal achievements, fulfillments and self gratifications. It is greater than who you want to marry, what career choice you choose, family and living your wildest dreams. It is imperative that you understand while in pursuit of this life paradox the silent truth that ultimately is revealed in the most darkest time in a person's life. It's not about you. If you wish to find your life purpose it must start with God. Finding life purpose requires removing you out of the suitcase. When you get rid of your wants and desires you will stop asking self-absorbed questions that only temporarily completes you. What do I want to do? What should I do with my life? What are my goals and ambitions? At the end of the searching, you must go back to the one who created you. You are made by God and for Gods purpose. It is amazing that in many people lives as they begin to seek God about who they are, they all find out what they love to do even as it relates to their employment, passions and desires, it all leads to who God has called them to be.

Everyday life gives us a glimpse as to what we are called to do in the earth, it's as if our life is everyday training for what God has equipped and designed us to do. Look at the story of David. The first time we see the young man David in the Bible is when the prophet Samuel comes to Jesse's house looking for the next king of Israel. King Saul had been rejected by God—though he still sat on the throne. God said in 1 Samuel 13 that He would remove the kingdom from Saul and give it to a "man after his own heart" (1 Samuel 13:13, 141 Samuel 13:13, 14). In chapter 16 Samuel went to Jesse's house looking to anoint the new king. David was Jesse's son and the youngest of eight brothers. Samuel looked over the other brothers and knew that God had not chosen any of them. Samuel asked Jesse if there were any more sons to consider. In 1 Samuel 16:11 Samuel said that he would eagerly wait until David came from the pasture where he was tending the sheep. Samuel anointed David as king even though he was still a young man. We don't know how old David was when this took place, but it is commonly believed that he was just a boy between the ages of 8 and 12. Though David had been chosen by God as a young boy, he did not become king over Judah and Israel until approximately 20 years later. When David was 30 years old he was anointed king over both the northern and southern tribes of Israel. God promised that the kingdom would be established in the family of David forever. Jesus, the king of eternity, was born from David's family. The kingdom of God was established in David. While David had many weaknesses in his life, he sought to be obedient and humble before God. Why is this story of great importance? Because I want you to see how you may not know who you are but it does not change who God has predestined you to be. David had no clue he was destined to be a king while tending to sheep. But his tending to sheep was training as to how to instruct and care for a kingdom that one day he would rule. What if the only items in David luggage only centered around where he saw himself at 12? What if he only prepared for what his father told him he would be and not whom God has prequalified him for? What if he only saw himself as a boy who would just tend to sheep but never recognized the kings anointing on his life. That is why it is of great importance to surround yourself with the right people. People that see you're potential and not just your job. Surround yourself with People that will invest in you today for your tomorrow. People that may know your history but trains you how to prepare for your future. Better yet, people that will show you how to pack a suitcase for where you are destined to go, not just for where you are now. The right person will celerbrate and confirm to you who you are while you're in the field taking care of sheep yet validate what others don't see in you as royal. David knew he was able to take care of sheep but didn't realize in the suitcase PREPARED BY God was a royal garment that qualified him to rule, guide, manage and takes care of a kingdom. He wore dirty rags in the field but David was being train to love the less lovable and instruct those that was stubborn as sheep in a palace. If you don't know who you are you will stay in a place of comfort simply because that's the only place you see yourself. When you have no clue as to who you are What's beneath you will be your passionate pursuit because that's the only place you have allowed people to tell you is your best. If you don't know who you are you want prepare for the day God has preordained for your promotion or the great reveal of your Destined Place. If you don't know who you are, you will not prepare or plan in the area of your calling. You will be investing time in the wrong area only to achieve less than Gods best for your life.

To know yourself can be intimidating when your not sure who's opinion of you really matters.

I convey this point because this is an area in your luggage that needs to be sorted through and either refolded or removed from your luggage. As we travel *through life, we experience living and encounter highs and lows while meeting a lot of people, many with different personalities and ways of living. Yet there are people in our lives who have always been there, such as family, to develop, train, guide, and love us. The funny observation is that the people closest to you can either make you or break you. They have such a powerful influence in your life. These people are a major factor in who you become, what you believe, and how you view your life and its development. The point of having luggage is you only pack what is needed or required for your journey. Some trips may require more than one suitcase, whereas an overnight trip may only require one bag. The point is to know where you're going and what is needed versus what is just taking up space. And if you're anything like me, you may tend to just throw in some items because you would rather be safe than sorry. The fewer unnecessary items you pack in your suitcase, the more space you add for the journey for your life as you evolve. This is the time you may need to unpack and open your awareness regarding your transparent self. This requires your attention to simply recognize whether you have learned any behaviors or picked up any habits or beliefs that were not your own.*

Please understand some behaviors or traditions are great, but you must recognize the ones that are not. People who do not know who they are will not learn how to embrace the new them because they have not taken the opportunity to see from their own perspective and do not have the maturity created by life lessons. The person you are today started as an impressionable little child and became an inquisitive young teenager who admired the beauty of growing up. In both your childhood and your teenage years, many people had the chance to impart within you their beliefs, traditions, opinions on various subjects and ways of life based on culture and experience. And most family and friends impart knowledge of their life to build you, inspire you, to develop your personality and character as a person. Stepping into the arena of womanhood, some women don't realize they have Grandma's personality, Mama's "deadbeat man"-hating attitude, their sister's baby-daddy drama, and ironically a favorite high-school teacher twist in their hip that they thought was drop-dead beautiful. Even as it relates to them as spiritual people, some have not taken the time to learn the religion they are a part of and have been since childhood. They grew up in church or a particular denomination and now know all the mechanics of church or religion. They know when to say the famous quotes like *"I'm blessed and highly favored."* They know when to buck, shout, and look deep, and sometimes, a few can just do it with closed eyes. And in a case like this, many have not built intimate relationships with themselves in which they are authentic or original.

People unknowingly become what and who they have watched for years. Whether you know it or not, your life has been an *"open womb."* Metaphorically the term *womb* refers to a place where something can generate or produce, meaning that you may have allowed yourself to conceive the traits of others and that you have produced some very similar qualities and characteristics beyond who you are. You have carried and produced seeds from people, and you have carried their opinions, thoughts, personalities, and behaviors for so long that you are past the impression stage. Until now, you have been impregnated by several individuals. You have come to a point in your life where it is time for birthing. It is time for you to come into your true identity, but sadly you realize you haven't been intimate with yourself or spent quality time getting to know yourself and what you like and love in a long time. However, you keep ending up carrying babies—that is, other people's distinctiveness that doesn't belong to you. You have loved someone else's life in cycles, and yet you keep saying you're unhappy with how your life is. Why? The answer to that question is awaiting your permission to give birth to the true you. It all starts by doing a luggage check. Unpack, refold, and leave out.

Two young ladies, named Alexis and Keisha, grew up in a small suburban community in Alabama. Both were children of parents in ministry and were very involved in their church. Alexis's dad was an attorney by career choice and minister by call. Keisha's dad, Mr. Jones, was a pastor by career choice and by call. From the time he could speak, Keisha's dad said that he knew he was called to preach the Gospels, minister, and preach some more. There was a running joke that even when Mr. Jones was proposing to Keisha's mom, he quoted John 3:16: *"For God so loved the world that He gave his only begotten son."* At the end of the proposal, he didn't give her a ring but asked her for an offering.

So Mr. Jones, without any question or hesitation, knew what he wanted to do in life. Now, the funny thing about this story is that Keisha was the only child of

Pastor Jones. All her life Keisha knew that Mr. Jones loved her but felt he never took interest in what her gifts were or thought to even show the slightest interest in what she enjoyed outside of the church. On the other hand, Alexis's dad, Mr. Wells, had always talked to Keisha and Alexis about ministry and college, asking them what their attention was geared toward regarding careers and what they wanted to do in life. At the same time, he focused on ministry. Alexis was a very bright girl, very smart and sharp. Her best friend, Keisha, was just as brilliant. They had different parents, but they felt like sisters. Keisha discovered she loved to read and sing, and Alexis loved reading and singing, too. But Alexis was very good at singing. Many said she had a sound of a soothing angel when she sang. As a matter of fact, it was her friend's idea to put her in a talent show to showcase her God-given talent. As the years passed, the two friends and their families grew closer, and the girls became closer than ever. They did everything together. They went to school together, went to the mall together. They families would dine together. You can say these girls were inseparable. It appeared they had genuine love for one another. If you saw one you saw the other.

Sadly the families started to grow apart the day Keisha and Alexis were getting ready to graduate from high school, and the talk was of what careers they were going to pursue. Well, for the Wells family, it was a no-brainer: Alexis desired and would pursue a career in law. And clearly Keisha was going to seminary school to continue the legacy of her father. Unfortunately, both families had a shock in their lives. Neither girl wanted to pursue or follow in her father's footsteps. Alexis decided she wanted to pursue a career in the medical field, and her parents were supportive of her decision. They all celebrated and partied like it was 1999, even though Alexis was planning to deviate from the traditions of her family. She enrolled in college to study medicine and took a part-time job singing at a nightclub. My, oh my, what a difference time makes- Alexis went from singing in the church choir to singing in the club. Now that's what you call doing your own thang. But, as always, her family supported her decision. Keisha decided she didn't want to follow in her father's footsteps, either. She wanted to become an attorney. She loved to read and do research and enjoyed the stimulation of courtroom drama. She knew, without a doubt, that was her heart's desire. She'd watched enough of television's Law & Order series to know she wanted to be an attorney and sat in on many of Mr. Jones's court hearings.

Why am I sharing this story with you? I want to open your eyes to the fact that the passion some people have for something in particular might not necessarily be someone else's ideal. Even though Pastor Jones was a very great father, he could not understand why his daughter did not want to be a pastor and carry on the family name in ministry. The pastor made such a fuss about it that he copycatted Fred G. Sanford of the hit television series Sanford & Son grabbing his chest and saying, "I'm coming to join you, honey," even though Mrs. Jones was still alive. The guilt, pressure, and rejection were so strong that Keisha changed her mind and enrolled in theology school to please her father.

When you decide to live someone else's dream
It becomes your nightmare.

The reason I wanted to share this story with you is to open your eyes to having luggage and packing it with other people's dreams for your life. You pack it with what someone else wants you to include. Some people desire to get married quickly because of the pressure to please others. Even though both fathers had great dreams for their daughters, the fathers' desires were very influential— until the wishes of the parent became the folded issue in a suitcase not suited for the daughter's journey. Mr. Jones was so strongly involved in his daughter's decision that she put aside her own heart's desire to please him. What I want for you to take from this story is that now that you are experiencing heartbreak or a divorce, don't allow the opinions of others cause you to make a life decision that you are not 100 percent certain is the best one for you.

Let me admonish you to love your life for you regardless of whether this is your first marriage or your fourth, your first heartbreak or the ninth. Keep making decisions that are right for you rather than living your life for others. The day you start to live for others is the day you abandon you. Living your life by your own desires results in you being the gift you are from God to the world. Even though the fathers in the previous story had their own ideas of the paths they wanted their daughters to take, at the end of the day, these girls had a choice—to be happy by pursuing their own dreams or to attempt to provide someone else with happiness. Don't allow pressure from other people to persuade your choices in life. The Bible says in Psalm 37:23 (KJV), "The steps of a good man [or woman] are ordered by the Lord."

Celebrating the new you is centered on what you feel is best for your life. Don't allow someone to talk you into going back to something or someone that brings you pain. The beauty of life is that when you're happy by your own standards, those around you are positively influenced by your sunny disposition. When you are the best you and are celebrating you, the freedom and the peace you feel spread to others. Don't worry about what went wrong or what you lost—think about what you are gaining. Or make a life choice to let go of a career or relationship that subtracts from your life. I always say that when things aren't adding up, start subtracting—that includes people, family and friends, and even career choices.

When you accept yourself—your dreams, your likes, your dislikes—it does not matter who agrees or disagrees. You must consistently live for you. You must live in your own truth. That's why so many people who have been in corporate America for years just walk away one day to open up a coffee shop or to travel abroad. What you are called to do, what you have been destined to pursue, what keeps you up at night, and what makes your baby leap is calling to you, and you must answer it, regardless of whether it makes sense to anyone else. Celebrate the original, true you, and the rest will follow.

I encourage you to seek God and ask Him to restore your joy as He gives you peace in this season of your life. This is your moment to collect all your pieces to the puzzle and love and live.

This is my prayer for you:

Dear Lord, today, as my sisters and brothers are on the road to restoration, recovery, healing, joy, peace, and surrender, I pray that You wrap them in Your arms. I ask that You mend every broken heart and repair the breach and damage they *feel internally, emotionally, and physically. Father, it is my prayer for them today that their hearts will be open to forgiveness as they submit to Your kingdom order. Heal the children, family members, and friends involved in this broken cistern. My Father, purify the impure places in their hearts and souls, and help them to come to terms with the cycles of their pasts so they choose not to live lives of hate, regret, and dysfunction. I ask You, God, to be the anchor of their souls as they lock themselves in You and Your will and process for their lives. Be the captain of their lifeboats and the wind that blows them in the right direction, upward and onward. Give them the capacity to love again and receive love from others, never settling for what they perceive as average, mediocre, or complacent. Father, I pray that You will help them see that a lesson learned is a key to a better life with You, Dear Lord, according to Psalms 126:5: "Those who sow in tears shall reap in joy." Let them know this is a great season for their lives. Help them to put their hands to the plow and work the gifts and talents You have placed in them. Also, allow them to be relevant in sharing their testimony to bring healing to others. Heavenly father, assist them in knowing their pain is the catalyst for victory and freedom, theirs and that of those they touch. Now, Father, I decree and declare, "No weapon formed against them shall prosper." I decree this moment n their loves will create a new hunger for your purpose for their lives so they will walk in the wholeness, joy and peace already given to them. I pray that in this time new doors of opportunity will be open and they will be able to recognize divine relationships- Relationships that will empower and fulfill their life. I decree they are the head and not the tail, a lender and not a borrower. I decree they have a fresh zeal, fresh hunger, and fresh excitement for their new life in you. I ask you father to open their eyes to see the new era and direction you are taking them to. A place of abundance and favor for them and those connected to them. Father, I decree the days of heaviness and frustration is over and they walk in a season of rest. Today, let your plan become there heartbeat and you love be their joy. And allow your spirit to guide them. Thank you father that because of you, they will be able to love again as they detach their souls from every illegal soul tide and relationship. I thank you that you hear our prayer and we seal it.*

In Jesus' name, Amen.

You can have a GODTASTIC future even if you've had what seems a bad past—your future is so much brighter than your today.

Your present is not permanent

After this, live.

I would like to dedicate this book to a man that taught me the true essence of Love and showed me how to be selfless. I pray I will be half the person you where as a parent, minister, and provider. To me you will always be the most amazing and loving father.

Jimmy Alvin Fomby Sr.

Always in my heart

About the Author

Melissa Williams is a minister and highly sought after conference and keynote speaker who travels the country to share her tagline, "God uses the flawed but chosen."

Williams experienced the tragedy of rape and the difficulties of teenage pregnancy and divorce and now lives to share her powerful testimony with those in need of help, encouragement, and direction.

She leads several effective community-based ministries, including the Melissa Williams Ministry, Daughters of Destiny Inc., The Youth Empowerment Outreach and Mentoring Program, and The Empowerment Learning Academy, where she is CEO.

Williams is the author of the best *selling Doubt and Destiny Don't Mix* and will soon release her first children's book, *The Things We Love and Lose.*

Williams lives in Birmingham, Alabama, and is the proud mother of three beautiful children: Cornelius, Dajia, and Angel.

Made in the USA
Columbia, SC
28 October 2024

44858172R00065